Charles E.

CONSERVATIVE SOCIAL AND INDUSTRIAL REFORM

A record of
Conservative legislation
between 1800 and 1974

With a Foreword by
THE RT. HON.
MARGARET THATCHER
MP

Conservative Political Centre

LONDON

CPC No 600

Published by the
CONSERVATIVE POLITICAL CENTRE
*32 Smith Square, London SW1P 3HH
and printed by
Morrison & Gibb Ltd,
London and Edinburgh*

*First published December 1947
Revised edition May 1977*

ISBN 0 85070 594 0

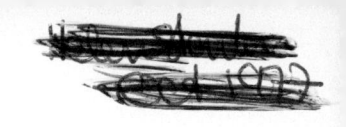

Charles E. Bellairs

CONSERVATIVE SOCIAL AND INDUSTRIAL REFORM

Contents

FOREWORD *by The Rt. Hon. Margaret Thatcher* MP   page 7

PART ONE

1800–1859. The revolt against *laissez-faire*	9
1860–1914. The condition of the people	15
1918–1939. Social reform between the wars	26
1940–1945. The four-year plan	44

PART TWO

Thirteen years of progress: 1951 to 1964   55
    The inheritance of failure from Labour: trade deficits; inflation; taxation; pensions and benefits; health and education; housing; rationing; nationalisation
    Thirteen years of record progress: prices and choice; earnings and pensions; savings; taxation; housing; education and health; the strength of the economy

PART THREE

The early 1970s: 1970 to 1974   89
    The legacy inherited from Labour: economic growth; unemployment; the standard of living; taxation; wage and price inflation; pensions and social welfare; housing

Summary of progress June 1970 to February 1974   91
    Growth of the economy; prices and income; taxation; pensions and benefits; education; health and welfare; housing; the environment

Appendix: The principal Conservative industrial and social Acts: 1800 to 1974   115

Index of persons   127

The author

CHARLES BELLAIRS OBE joined the Conservative Research Department in 1946. He was head of its Home Affairs section from 1963 until the beginning of this year, and is now an Assistant Director.

Foreword

by The Rt. Hon. Margaret Thatcher MP

IT IS A FAMILIAR TRUISM to say that the Conservative Party has been in existence much longer than the Labour Party; or that it has been much more deeply and constructively involved in the history of our country. It is a less familiar proposition that Conservative concern for and involvement in what we nowadays call welfare politics has been much more marked, and much more effective, than that of any rival party.

Take, for example, the nineteenth century, which Mr Bellairs discusses in so illuminating a fashion in this pamphlet.

Practically every measure of social amelioration passed through Parliament in the nineteenth century was passed by Conservatives, often against bitter and entrenched Liberal opposition. The greatest social reformer of the period was the Tory, Lord Shaftesbury. And while its rivals concentrated solely on the propagation of unlimited economic competition – the so-called policy of *laissez-faire* – whatever the human cost to workers and their dependants, it was the Tories who, throughout the century, sought to mitigate the rigours and the consequences of the Industrial Revolution.

Nor is the picture presented by our own century as markedly different as it might appear on the surface. The Socialists certainly make a great parade of their concern for the deprived of the community but the fact of the matter is that the consequences of their overall economic policies bear most heavily on those least able to look after themselves.

Labour is the party that declares, again and again, its commitment to nationalisation, State control of our lives and the elimination of competition and variety. Policies designed to serve these ends invariably produce inflation, instability and uncertainty. It is precisely the dramatic lurches of the economy under Socialist governments that bear most hardly on the old, the sick and the poor. It is stability, above all, which the pensioner needs. It is a steady provision, above all, which the patients of successive generations require. And it is only in economic conditions which are orderly that the poor can hope for the opportunity to improve their lot.

But, beyond Socialist incompetence, which all clients of the Welfare State in particular, have felt in the last decade, there is a greater threat. Labour's economic programme – which is not yet completed, but towards which the Government is marching as fast as an uncertain parliamentary situation and pressure from our overseas creditors will allow them – envisages, ultimately, complete governmental control over the economy, industry, and wide swathes of our national life. This, as we have seen in other Socialist countries, is a prescription for the ending of economic growth, and thus the ending of improvements in welfare. Moreover, a dominant state is an insensitive state: the cry of the weak and the needy is the last to be heard by all-powerful ministers. Once everything is provided and controlled by the State, the voice of the individual is silenced, the ability to choose eliminated.

I believe that only an economy based on free enterprise can generate the wealth to provide for our needs and, in this case, particularly the needs of the more unfortunate and deprived among us. I believe that only the Conservative principles of thrift and industry will provide that stability of provision which alone can provide shelter for the vulnerable. And I believe that only a free society can hope to be a truly compassionate one. Mr Bellairs sets out the record on all these matters with admirable clarity and, in the process, has struck a telling blow against the uncaring dogmas of Socialism.

Margaret W. Thatcher

PART ONE

1800–1859. The revolt against *laissez faire*

THE PERIOD 1800–1860 was one of the most notable periods in the history of social reform in this country.

At the beginning of the century, the labour conditions of women and children employed in factories were appalling. Many of the women and young children worked up to sixteen hours a day, and there was no provision for schooling. The housing conditions of the poor were in urgent need of improvement and nearly all the large cities were infested with slum areas. By 1860 the efforts of Conservative statesmen had succeeded in placing on the statute book legislation which laid the foundations of social progress.

1802

A Conservative government under Henry Addington passed the first ameliorative factory act in 1802. This measure reduced the work of children and women in mills and factories to twelve hours a day, made night-work illegal, required a certain amount of education for apprentices and gave power to magistrates to appoint visitors to children apprenticed by poor-law guardians.

1819

In 1819, the Conservative government of Lord Liverpool passed a second act under which no children under nine were allowed to work in the cotton mills.

1824

The year 1824 saw the legalisation of trade unions. Under the old penal laws directed against combination it was illegal for workmen to combine to secure a reduction in the hours of labour or an increase in wages and such combination was treated as a criminal offence and called, in English law, conspiracy. In 1820 the Conservative government of Lord Liverpool appointed a royal commission to inquire into the working of these laws and in 1824 a Conservative Act was passed repealing the previous anti-combination laws and establishing the workers' right to combine and form trade unions. This measure was described in Sidney and Beatrice Webb's *History of Trade Unionism* as 'the most impressive event in the early history of the trade union movement'.

1831

Very early in time are the measures which entitled working men to receive the wages of their labour in good current coin of the realm. The **Truck Acts,** as they were called, marked an important stage in the social advance and material progress of the workers, and they were all passed either by Conservative governments or as a direct result of Conservative pressure.

Under the truck system employers paid their workmen not in money but in goods, keeping in some cases stores where these goods were issued at exorbitant prices, and insisting very often on labour being paid by articles which the working man and his family did not want. In *Sybil*, Benjamin Disraeli drew a startling picture of the evils of this system, the facts of which he had carefully studied. An effort was made in 1830 to remedy these evils but owing largely to the opposition of the Liberals of the day, the bill had not passed through all its stages when Parliament was dissolved.

The hostile attitude of the Liberals to Conservative attempts to end the iniquitous truck system can be judged from the remark by the then Liberal MP for Worcester who asserted that 'to put an end to the truck system would, in many cases, put an end to the employment of the workmen altogether'.

Finally in 1831 two Acts received the Royal Assent. The first repealed all the existing enactments on the subject of truck and the second provided that workmen in a number of the principal industries must receive payment in the current coin of the realm.

Sir Robert Peel, in advocating the abolition of the truck system, declared that he did so 'being convinced that no system was so calculated to destroy the independence of workmen'.

1832

During 1832, when a Liberal government was in office, numerous petitions 'for the abolition of Infant Slavery in Factories' were presented to Parliament. In 1832, a bill for the amelioration of child labour in factories by limiting the hours of work of all between the ages of nine and eighteen to ten hours a day was introduced by Michael Sadler, Conservative MP for Newark, and given a second reading in the House of Commons on condition that a select committee should examine the whole question. This measure was designed to protect not only children in cotton mills but also in textile factories. Sadler was chairman of the committee, which was subsequently appointed, and from its endeavours came the historic report of 1831–1832, known as Sadler's Report, 'ordered by the House of Commons to be printed, August 8, 1832'. This report revealed a terrible state of cruelty, misery and disease.

In the General Election of 1832, however, which resulted once again in the return of a Liberal government, Sadler was defeated by his Liberal opponent. The cause of the children was immediately taken up by another Conservative statesman, Lord Ashley, subsequently the Earl of Shaftesbury. On 3rd February 1833, Shaftesbury gave notice of a motion for the renewal of Sadler's Bill and the following month he was afforded a first reading of his measure. Shaftesbury's Bill was almost identical with Sadler's and its chief provisions were that no child was to be employed under nine years of age, that no person under eighteen should be engaged more than ten hours a day and that no person under twenty-one was to be employed at night. The Liberal government, however, claimed that Sadler's Report had been partial to workers and unfair to manufacturers and refused to proceed with legislation without further evidence. Accordingly a new commission was appointed, which although not so outspoken as the Sadler Report, nevertheless revealed valuable data regarding the ill-treatment of children. As a result of this commission's report an Act, which was based on the original measure introduced by Shaftesbury, became law in 1833. Under this Act, the labour of children under thirteen was limited to eight hours a day, and that of children under nine was prohibited. It was further enacted that persons under eighteen should never be obliged to work more than twelve hours in one day or sixty-nine hours a week. Government inspection was established, night work for persons under eighteen was prohibited, a surgeon's certificate of fitness for work was required in the case of children and provision was made for their education.

1842

The General Election of 1841 resulted in the return of a Conservative administration under Sir Robert Peel. One of the first Acts of this government was the **Coal Regulations Act,** of 1842, which was the first major reform dealing with the mining industry. This Act was largely due to the inspiration of Shaftesbury by whose exertions a royal commission had been appointed in 1840, which brought to light the hideous system whereby boys and girls of six years old were sent into the mines and worked in darkness for twelve hours a day. As a result of the findings of this commission the 1842 Act was passed, which entirely put a stop to the underground employment of women and of boys under ten years of age and provided for the appointment of inspectors to secure that it should be carried out.

Considerable opposition to this measure came from the Liberals, notably Mr Bright.

1843

In 1843 Shaftesbury founded his Ragged School Movement. There were in London during this period many children running wild, whose parents were dead or missing and who knew no law nor settled home. They slept under the arches or anywhere else they could find and scraped out some sort of existence by selling matches and thieving.

Through his Ragged School Movement Shaftesbury gave destitute boys and girls some prospect and purpose in life by providing them with the rudiments of education; he also organised schemes for training and emigration. Today the Shaftesbury Homes, where thousands of boys and girls have been trained for work at home and overseas, stand as a lasting monument to the work of this great Conservative statesman, who dedicated his life to the service of his country's poor. Charles Dickens, who did so much to awaken the social conscience of the British people, has testified to the magnificent work achieved by the Ragged School Movement.

1844

In 1844 Sir Robert Peel's Conservative government passed an Act by which the hours of women and young persons between twelve and eighteen were limited to twelve hours a day, or sixty-nine a week, and the minimum age of child labour reduced to eight years. It was enacted that no child under eighteen should be employed more than ten hours and the half-time system was established.

The most active enemies of this measure were two Liberals. Mr John Bright who described it as 'miserable legislation on principles false and mischievous' and Lord Brougham, who asked sarcastically why it was not also proposed to limit the hours of 'washerwomen and wet-nurses'.

1845

The principle that it is the duty of the Government to look after the health and conditions of the people was first applied in 1845 by the

Conservative administration of Sir Robert Peel when the Board of Supervision – the forerunner of the subsequent Ministry of Health – was established.

In 1834 Shaftesbury had been made Chairman of the Board of Commissioners in Lunacy and he had brought to light serious abuses in the treatment of the insane. During this period lunacy was interpreted as a pernicious form of demon possession, and was considered outside the scope of medical treatment, consequently repellent tortures were devised to exorcise these 'evil spirits' supposed to reign with maniacal rage over the victim's mind.

In 1845 two measures were passed by Sir Robert Peel's government under which county asylums were erected and prompt medical treatment was ensured. It was also provided that a certificate of insanity, signed by two disinterested doctors, had to be presented before any person was confined to an asylum. In fact the whole treatment of lunacy was humanised and lifted out of the atmosphere of profits into that of curative effort and civic responsibility.

1847

In 1847 after their long political struggle against Liberal opposition the Conservatives succeeded in realising their ambition for a ten-hour day. The **Ten Hours Act** limited the normal working hours for all young persons under eighteen and all women workers in textile factories to fifty-eight a week. This measure was bitterly opposed by certain Liberals, notably Mr Cobden and Mr Bright.

1851

The Lodging-Houses Acts of 1851, which were both passed at the insistence of Lord Shaftesbury, marked the first attempt of the legislature to grapple with the question of unhealthy dwellings. It is interesting to note that, while Lord Shaftesbury made one of his last speeches in the House of Commons in asking leave to bring in the Lodging-Houses Bill, his first public appearance in the House of Lords was when, in the same year, he moved its second reading. In his speech in the Upper House, Lord Shaftesbury quoted several almost incredible instances of filth, wretchedness and overcrowding in the dwellings of the very poor.

The **Common Lodging-Houses Act**, which was described by Charles Dickens as 'the best measure ever passed in Parliament,' provided that all such lodging-houses should be registered and that no lodgers were to be kept until the houses had been inspected and opened by an officer of the local authority. The local authority was given power to make regulations for common lodging-houses, and to exact penalties for breaches of regulations. Regular cleansing and whitewashing were enforced and it was rendered compulsory for the keeper of a lodging-house to give immediate notice of any case of fever or infectious disease in the house to the local authority, to the Poor Law medical officer and to the relieving officer.

The **Lodging-Houses Act** of the same year empowered borough councils and local boards to erect lodging-houses or to purchase existing lodging-houses, and to manage them, making by-laws for charges, management, etc. Such lodging-houses were under the inspection of the local boards of health.

1854

An incident in the life of Lord Shaftesbury worthy of recording is in connection with the Crimean war. In 1854 on hearing about the appalling conditions of our soldiers in the Crimea, Lord Shaftesbury set about organising a medical expedition to go out at once to the Middle East. Florence Nightingale afterwards declared that this expedition saved the British Army.

1859

A further step in the interest of trade unionism was taken by the Conservative government of Lord Derby, which in 1859, legalised peaceful picketing when *really* peaceful. The effect of this was destroyed by subsequent legislation for which the Conservatives were not responsible but the right was restored by the Conservatives in 1875.

1860–1914. The condition of the people

1860

During the period 1860 to 1866 when the Liberals were in office little attempt was made to improve the conditions of the workers.

1866

In 1866, however, when a Conservative government under Lord Derby returned to office, factory legislation took a fresh start and an Act was passed dealing with uncleanliness, inadequate ventilation, and overcrowding in factories.

1867

In 1867, the Conservatives extended the provisions of the 1866 Act to blast-furnaces, copper mills, iron foundries, machinery works, the paper, glass, tobacco, printing and bookbinding trades and to all other works employing over fifty operatives. By this Act 1,500,000 women and children were admitted to the benefits of the factory laws.

In the same year the Conservatives passed an Act regulating the hours of women workers in every workshop. The employment of children under eight was prohibited, that of those over eight limited to six and a half hours daily and that of young persons under thirteen to twelve hours, with one and a half for meals. In addition work on Sunday or Saturday afternoons was forbidden, and every working child was obliged to attend school for at least ten hours a week.

Prior to 1867, a workman could be summarily imprisoned for breaking a contract of employment. The employer on the other hand could not be imprisoned for breaking faith with his workman but was only subject to a pecuniary penalty.

The workman, however, could be arrested without any charge being served upon him, brought summarily before one magistrate and tried in private, and if he were convicted the magistrate was obliged to send him to jail, there being no option of a fine.

By the Conservative government's **Master and Servant Act** of 1867, the following important changes were made:

(*a*) The workman could no longer be summarily arrested but must have a summons or charge served upon him.

(*b*) The trial must be in public, and before two Justices or the Sheriff.

(*c*) The workman must give evidence on his own behalf.

(*d*) The court must impose a fine in the first instance instead of sending the offender to jail, and imprisonment could follow only on a failure to recover the fine.

In 1872 Benjamin Disraeli declared that 'the first consideration of a Minister should be the health of the people'. It is, therefore, particularly fitting that one of the earliest Acts of his first administration in 1867 was to pass the **Public Health (Scotland) Act** under which sanitary inspectors and medical officers were first instituted. Power was given to local authorities to stop nuisances, and better sanitation was enforced throughout Scotland.

In the field of electoral reform, the **Reform Act** of 1867 gave the vote to the workers who were householders in towns. This measure increased the electorate by nearly one million.

1868

The General Election of 1868 resulted in a large Liberal majority of 100 and the return of a Liberal administration under Mr Gladstone.

The only notable Act passed during this period was the Education Act of 1870, which established the Board Schools. This Act was, however, defective in many ways since it did not make education compulsory, and there was no provision for the payment of fees when the parent was unable to meet them. Nevertheless, in spite of these shortcomings, this measure did represent an advance in the right direction and its successful passage was due to the aid which the Conservatives gave the Government in resisting opposition from certain liberal sections, a fact which was acknowledged by Mr W. M. Forster, the author of the bill.

In 1874, in spite of the bribe offered by Mr Gladstone's proposal for the abolition of the income tax, a Conservative government under Disraeli was returned to power.

Disraeli's government held office until 1880 and one of its chief features was the attention given to practical social legislation.

In his famous speech at the Crystal Palace on 24th June 1872,

Disraeli laid it down that the Conservative Party had three great objects:

(*a*) To maintain our Institutions.

(*b*) To uphold the Empire.

(*c*) To elevate the condition of the People.

1874

In pursuance of Disraeli's aim to elevate the condition of the people, one of the first acts of his second administration was to pass a **Factories Act** which reduced the working hours of women and young persons to fifty-six hours per week, and prevented their continuous employment for more than four and a half hours. The minimum age for children was raised from eight to ten and an educational certificate was required.

1875

The health of the nation was also the object of special attention by this government, which in 1875 passed the **Public Health Act** extending to England the benefits conferred on Scotland by the measure passed in 1867 by Disraeli's first government. This Act laid the foundations of public health administration today. It was bitterly opposed by the Liberals who derided it as 'a policy of sewage'.

Mr Disraeli's cry had been 'Pure air, pure water, the inspection of unhealthy habitations, the prevention of the adulteration of food.' Having done much to accomplish the first three of these objectives, he took up the last also in 1875, and passed the **Sale of Food and Drugs Act.**

This measure prohibited the mixing of injurious ingredients with articles of food or with drugs. Provision was also made for the appointment of analysts and a special provision was made whereby all tea had to be examined by a customs official on importation, and when in the opinion of the analyst it was unfit for food, the tea had to be destroyed.

Although the Master and Servant Act of 1867 had effected a great improvement in the state of the law as between master and servant, breach of contract by a servant still remained a criminal offence. Nothing was done by the Gladstone ministry during its five years' tenure of office, but shortly after being returned to power Disraeli's government appointed a royal commission to inquire into this question. As soon as that commission had reported, Mr Cross, the Conservative Home Secretary, introduced the **Employers' and Work-**

men's Act, 1875, which finally placed employers and employed on an equal footing before the law. Power was still left to the courts of law to deal in a summary way with disputes between masters and workmen but it was expressly declared that such a case 'shall not be deemed to be a criminal proceeding,' and that for the purposes of this Act the court 'shall be deemed to be a court of civil jurisdiction'.

The law of conspiracy was another law which operated very harshly towards the workers since conduct which was entirely innocent if done by one person, might amount to the crime of conspiracy if a number of people agreed to follow the same line of action. This evil was remedied by the **Conspiracy Act,** of 1875, which finally established the right to strike by providing that 'an agreement or combination by one or more persons to do, or procure to be done, any act in contemplation or furtherance of a trade dispute between employers and workmen, shall not be indictable as a conspiracy if such act committed by one person would not be punishable as a crime'. At the Trade Union Congress of 1875 a vote of thanks was passed to Mr Cross for carrying through this Act, and one member of the TUC, Mr Odger, said the Home Secretary had accorded them 'the greatest boon ever given to the sons of toil'.

In the Webb's *History of Trade Unionism* the effect of this measure was summarised as follows: 'The legalisation of trade unions was completed by the legal recognition of their methods. Collective bargaining, in short, with all its necessary accompaniments, was firmly recognised by the law of the land'.

At this point in the development of trade unionism it is appropriate to recall the following definition of a trade union contained in the same book: 'a continuous association of wage-earners for the purpose of maintaining or improving the conditions of their working lives'.

The year 1875 saw the end of the iniquitous practice whereby small children were employed as climbing boys in the sweeping of chimneys. Year after year children were bought and sold to a life of dirt and suffering and sometimes a child or two from their number gained local notoriety by being suffocated in a flue. It will be remembered that in 1863, Charles Kingsley wrote *Water Babies*, making the small, ill-treated, climbing-boy, Tom, its central figure. A continuous campaign had been carried on against the practice of employing climbing-boys by Lord Shaftesbury but, although made illegal, it still persisted. It was not until 1875 that these scandals were brought to an end by a Conservative Act under which every master sweep had to be licensed annually, the licence being withheld if the law had been in any way contravened.

Disraeli's government made the first attempt to improve the housing conditions of the very poor. Under the **Artisan's Dwellings Act** public authorities were called in to remedy the defects of private dwelling houses. By its provisions local authorities were empowered to remove existing buildings for sanitary reasons and replace them by others, the new buildings to be devoted to the use of workers. True to his rigid economic theory, the well-known Liberal, Mr Fawcett, scoffed at the proposal and asked why Parliament should facilitate the housing of working men and not that of dukes? But the workers themselves and the general public welcomed this measure dealing with the rookeries which disgraced our urban civilisation, and made decent life almost impossible for those who lived in them. Mr Joseph Chamberlain, shortly after the passing of this Act, stated that it had 'done more for the town of Birmingham than had been done in the twenty preceding years of Liberal legislation'.

Movements for the promotion of thrift and mutual help have always received the most sympathetic support and help from Conservative governments and in 1875 the **Friendly Societies Act** was passed which struck a mean between the extremes of too great state interference and of insufficient protection. This measure left the societies with a wide measure of self-management but insured the adoption of sound rules, effective audit, and rates of payment sufficient to maintain solvency. In fact, the Friendly Societies, and the people's savings, were established on a satisfactory basis.

1876

Although the first Act by which co-operative societies were recognised as such was passed in 1852 by Lord Derby's Conservative administration, it was not until 1876 that these societies were placed on the footing on which they now stand. This measure passed by Disraeli's government conferred many important privileges on these societies. Chief amongst these was that they now became corporations, and could sue and be sued, and hold land in their own name, and not in the names of trustees as was formerly the case. This act also empowered co-operative societies to carry on the business of banking.

In 1876 the government passed the **Merchant Shipping Act,** which provided for the safety and protection of seamen. Under it major powers were given to the Board of Trade to detain unsafe ships, and provision was made for the appointment of detaining officers at ports, and for courts of survey for appeals. The distinct marking of deck and load lines was enforced and Wreck Commissioners were appointed to investigate into shipping casualties. From 1876 to 1890 some 701 ships were detained under the provisions of this Act as unsafe on account of defects in the hull or equipment, and 562 for faults in loading. We can thus form some idea of the lives saved by this measure.

The Conservative **Education Act** of 1876 made education compulsory throughout England and remedied many defects in the existing education system. The employment of young children in such a way as to interfere with their education was prohibited and provision was made for the payment of the fees for children of poor parents.

The enormous progress achieved under Conservative legislation so impressed Mr A. Macdonald, who termed himself a Liberal and Labour MP, that in a speech during 1879 he declared: 'Conservatives have done more for the working classes in five years than the Liberals have in fifty'.

1880–1885

Under the Liberal government of Mr Gladstone, which succeeded to office in 1880, there was comparatively little attempt to continue the work of the Disraeli administration in social reform.

1885

In 1885, a Conservative administration under Lord Salisbury came into power, but held office for only six months.

1886

Following upon its resignation, Mr Gladstone once again became Prime Minister. Necessarily, in view of the government's dependence upon the Irish Nationalist vote, Home Rule occupied the predominant place in the legislative programme. The Liberal Party, however, were utterly split on this question and when the Home Rule Bill was rejected on 7th June 1886, a General Election followed which resulted in the return of a second Conservative administration under Lord Salisbury; its record was one of peace abroad and progress at home.

1887

One of the first subjects taken in hand by this government was the provision of regulations to ensure the safety of mineworkers. The **Mines Regulation Act,** 1887, was one of the greatest measures ever passed for the benefit of miners and was known as the Miner's Charter. This measure which laid the foundation of all modern mining regulations was opposed by the Liberals who assumed an attitude not far removed from open obstruction. Under the Act the miners were given the right to appoint their own checkweighmen. It also dealt with the supply of timber, distance between props, duties of roadmen and inspectors, and other matters relating to the safety of mineworkers. A Labour MP, Mr Burt, described it as 'the greatest measure of its kind that had ever yet been passed by a British Government'.

The year 1887 saw the complete break-up of the iniquitous truck system. Under the **Truck Amendment Act** of that year, the previous Truck Acts were made applicable to all workmen with the exception of agricultural labourers, to whom it was often convenient to receive payment in kind.

In the same year the government **Allotments Act,** which first gave compulsory powers to municipal corporations, the forerunners of county councils, to secure land for allotments and which provided compensation to tenants for crops when they gave them up, was passed.

1888

The **Local Government Act** of this year created the county councils and from these bodies the modern structure of local government has been built up.

1889

To protect the health of workers in the cotton industry from the effects of damp and excessive moisture, regulations were made under the **Cotton Cloth Factory Act,** 1889.

1890

Owing to pressure from Lord Salisbury a royal commission on housing had been appointed in 1874. As a result of the findings of this commission the Salisbury administration passed in 1890 the important **Housing of the Working Classes Act,** which brought up to date all previous legislation dealing with the housing of the working classes.

1891

Free education was brought within the reach of almost every family in England by the Conservative Act of 1891, which provided special government grants for schools willing to abolish fees for children between three and fifteen years of age.

The **Factory and Workshop Act** of 1891 was another important measure. It made new and stringent regulations applicable to all workshops, which could be enforced by the local authority or the Home Office in case of default. Special rules were provided against dangerous machinery, faulty premises or ventilation and insufficient means of escape from fire. The limits of hours for women were made more certain and enforceable and the future employment of children under eleven was prohibited after 1892.

1892

A very successful **Small Holding Act** was passed in 1892 which gave powers to county councils where there was a demand for small holdings, to acquire land which came into the market.

The Conservative **Shop Hours Regulation Act,** of 1892, was the first attempt to limit the working hours of shop assistants under eighteen to seventy-four a week, including meal times.

1895

At the General Election of 1892 the Liberal Gladstone-Rosebery government was returned and remained in power until 1895, when the General Election resulted in a Conservative victory and the formation of Lord Salisbury's third and last administration.

The Conservative Party now remained in office for upwards of ten years. There were two Parliaments and two administrations, for Lord Salisbury was succeeded by Mr Balfour in July 1902.

The period 1895 to 1905 was one of steady and continual social reform.

1897

The **Workmen's Compensation Act,** 1897, introduced the important principle that employers were liable to pay compensation to workers or their dependants in case of accidents, fatal or otherwise. This measure imposed upon employers in certain industries, chosen on the grounds of their being the most dangerous, liability to give compensation in every case of 'personal injury arising out of and in the course of the employment of the workman'. Compensation consisted of half wages so long as the man was rendered unfit for his employment by the accident, but was only to apply to incapacity lasting more than two weeks. In the case of death a lump sum not exceeding £300 was payable to the workman's dependents. This measure benefited some six million workers and the industries concerned were railways, factories, mines, quarries, engineering works and buildings exceeding 30 feet in height where scaffolding was being used or on which machinery driven by mechanical power was being operated. This Act brought a chorus of appreciation from the ranks of Socialist MPs. One MP, Mr G. W. Barnes, described it as being 'one of the best pieces of social legislation which has been placed on the statute book in years'.

Another MP, Mr S. A. Thomas, in a speech to his constituents expressed the opinion that during the ten years he had the honour to represent them in Parliament he did not remember any other social reform in the House of Commons which equalled the Compensation Act in its value to the working men of this country.

1899

A further Act was passed in 1899 improving the lot of shop assistants. This measure required all shops employing 'female assistants' to provide seats in the proportion of one to every three persons.

An important housing measure was passed in 1899 under which local authorities were enabled to buy land for the erection of workmen's dwellings either within or outside their respective areas.

1900

The **Workmen's Compensation Amendment Act** of this year brought agricultural workers within the scope of workmen's compensation.

1901

In 1901, the government passed the **Factories and Workshop Act.** This measure, which was largely the work of the Home Secretary, Mr C. T. Ritchie, improved and brought up to date the whole of the law relating to factories and workshops. For the first time special provision was made for the safety of steam-boilers and new powers were given to guarantee means of escape in case of fire. In addition the employment of children under twelve was prohibited.

In his Presidential address to the Trades Union Congress, at Swansea in 1901, Mr C. W. Bowerman, Labour MP for Deptford, described this measure as 'in all respects the most comprehensive work of this kind yet placed on the statute book'.

1902

The **Education Act** of this year laid the foundation of popular education as we know it today. This measure placed the national system of state provided and voluntary schools on a permanent basis under local education authorities in place of the former board schools and gave them power to provide adequate facilities for secondary and technical schools.

1904

In 1904 a further **Shops Act** was passed empowering local authorities under certain conditions to effect the closing of shops early enough to assure the shorter working day.

This measure prevented the practice whereby women assistants were often kept on duty for 84 or 85 hours a week.

1905

The **Unemployed Workmen Act,** which was largely the work of Mr Walter Long, was the first measure to give serious attention to the question of unemployment. In speaking of this Act, which established distress committees to assist in the finding of work for unemployed persons, the well-known Labour leader, Mr Will Crooks, MP, said: 'Many and many a home had been kept which would have been broken up today but for that Act'.

The Socialist statesman, Mr Ramsay MacDonald, described this measure as 'one of the most courageous pieces of statesmanship of our generation'.

On 5th December 1905, the Conservative administration was succeeded by a Liberal government first under Sir Henry Campbell-Bannerman and then from April 1908, under Mr Asquith. Political events from 1905 to 1914 were largely submerged by the nearer tragedy of war, and Germany grew to dominate foreign policy everywhere.

1908

In the domestic sphere this period was in the main one of acute political controversy. There were, however, certain measures which commanded general support. The first was the Old Age Pensions Act, 1908, under which non-contributory old age pensions on a needs basis were first given at the age of seventy. The passing of this Act ended a long period of Conservative agitation to popularise old age pensions. As early as 1899 a largely Conservative committee, presided over by Mr Henry Chaplin, made a study of the whole question of old age pensions and its report formed the basis of the 1908 Act. One of the earliest advocates of this much-needed reform was Mr Joseph Chamberlain, and Mr Lloyd George himself testified that Mr. Chamberlain had done more than anybody else to popularise the idea of old age pensions.

In the field of education, the Liberal government adopted a partisan spirit which made progress impossible. Three measures were introduced which were dictated largely by hostility towards denominational education, and had to be dropped.

Licensing was another problem taken up by the government and which caused such acute controversy that it had to be dropped. In 1908, Mr Asquith introduced a Licensing Bill which provided for the suppression of 30,000 on-licences. This measure, however, found little favour and after having been defeated in the House of Lords, was dropped.

1911

In 1911 Mr Winston Churchill was one of Mr Lloyd George's principal lieutenants in securing the passage of the National Insurance Act of that year and was responsible for recommending to the House of Commons the unemployment insurance proposals of that Act.

Health insurance was initiated by this measure which also introduced unemployment insurance for a limited number of trades and was warmly welcomed by the Conservative Party.

1918–1939. Social reform between the wars

1918

Immediately after the Armistice came the General Election of December 1918, which resulted in the return of Mr Lloyd George's coalition government, in which the Conservatives were in the majority.

There was as much need for unity after the 1914–1918 war as there had been during it. This fact was recognized by Conservatives and Liberals who followed Mr Lloyd George and continued the coalition which the war had produced. The main opposition came from the Labour Party. Knowing the difficulties that faced the government abroad and at home where the whole economic and industrial machinery was running abnormally, and the urgent need was to bring it back to a normal movement, the Labour Party determined to obstruct the government to the utmost of its power. Their main weapon was the trade union organisation, which they controlled, and their plan was to use this industrial machine for political ends. The struggle to maintain the high wartime wages was bound to come soon after the conclusion of the peace and it was immediately linked by the Labour Party to the political demand for nationalisation. As a result industrial unrest fomented by Socialist agitators was prevalent and the recovery of the country was retarded, thereby causing considerable unemployment and distress.

The problem of the ex-service man naturally claimed special attention and the government reached a scale of pensions which was the highest rate in Europe. Grants were also provided for educational and industrial training.

The **Representation of the People Act,** 1918, established a democratic franchise by extending the electorate from $5\frac{1}{2}$ millions to 21 millions and giving 9 million women the vote for the first time.

The **Maternity and Child Welfare Act,** which originated maternity and child welfare work by local authorities, was passed in the same year.

A notable advance was made in the field of education by the **Education Act,** 1918, which finally abolished fees for elementary education in all government-aided schools. A great merit of this measure, known as the Fisher Act, was that it avoided all religious controversy.

The **Parliament (Qualification of Women) Act**, 1918, gave women the right to sit in the House of Commons.

1919

Under the **Ministry of Health Act** of this year the local Government Board ceased to exist and the Ministry of Health was created in its place.

The **Old Age Pensions Act**, 1919, increased the pension from the pre-war figure of 5s to 10s (25p–50p) a week.

The **Sex Disqualification (Removal) Act**, 1919, removed many barriers to women's participation in public life and gave women the right to sit on juries, and to take part in the administration of justice by being appointed Justices of the Peace.

1920

The **Unemployment Insurance Act**, 1920, made unemployment insurance of general application, except in regard to agriculture and domestic service. As a result the scope of unemployment insurance was extended from application to four million workers to twelve million workers.

Under the **Employment of Women and Children Act**, 1920, no child under fourteen was allowed to be employed in any industrial undertaking and night work for persons under eighteen and women was prohibited, except in special circumstances.

The conditions of the blind were vastly improved by the **Blind Persons Act**, 1920. Under this measure an old age pension was provided at the age of fifty instead of seventy to persons so blind as to be unable to perform work for which eyesight is essential. Power was also given to local authorities to provide and maintain or contribute towards the provision and maintenance of workshops, hostels, homes and other places for the reception of blind persons.

1921

Conservatives have always held that the dumping of goods made abroad under unfair conditions, such as sweated labour or excessive hours, was an injustice to British workers who make similar articles in this country and, in 1921, the Coalition Government passed a temporary measure, the **Safeguarding of Industries Act,** which introduced safeguarding duties on a limited number of articles, mainly of vital importance to the nation.

The **Trade Facilities Act** of this year authorised the Treasury to guarantee the repayment of loans to be applied towards the carrying out of capital undertakings. This original Act was continued and amended by later measures in 1925 and 1926.

1922

In October 1922, Mr Lloyd George's coalition government came to an end and at the General Election which followed, the Conservative Party, under the leadership of Mr Bonar Law, was returned to office with a majority of 75 over all other parties.

1923

The new government had not been long in office, when in May 1923, increasing ill-health obliged Mr Bonar Law to resign. Mr Stanley Baldwin then became the new Conservative Prime Minister until the General Election of November 1923, which resulted in the return of a Socialist government under Mr Ramsay MacDonald.

Although this Conservative administration was short-lived it passed a number of Acts which were of great value to the community.

Rates on agricultural land were reduced to one-quarter and the **Agricultural Credits Act** was passed to remedy the hardship incurred by farmers who purchased their farms between 1917 and 1921 relying on the assurances of the Corn Production Acts, which were repealed in 1921.

The **Housing Act,** 1923, known as the Neville Chamberlain Act, was the first really practical measure to overcome the housing shortage created by the cessation of building during the war. As a result of this Act when the Conservative Party returned to power (1924–1929) all previous housing records were broken.

A **Rent Restriction Act** was also passed in 1923 to protect working-class tenants against rent profiteering during the after-war housing shortage.

The **Workmen's Compensation Act,** 1923, provided for increased scales of workmen's compensation. In addition certain special classes such as shore fishermen, taxicab drivers, casual workers for the purposes of any game or recreation, and employees on ships were brought into the scheme for the first time.

Millions of policy-holders were protected by the **Industrial Insurance Act,** 1923, which carried out the recommendations of a departmental committee appointed in 1919 to inquire into the business carried on by industrial assurance companies. The chief features of this reform were:

- (*a*) definition of industrial assurance was extended to cover human life assurance of every form so long as premiums were collected at intervals of less than two months;
- (*b*) control of all such agencies to be vested in the Chief Registrar of Friendly Societies, who was in future to be known as the Industrial Assurance Commissioner;
- (*c*) illegal policies, that is, policies issued to persons having no insurable interest in the life of the insured were dealt with by fining the company and requiring the return of premiums paid;
- (*d*) lapsed policy-holders were entitled to receive a fully-paid policy representing the actuarial value of the premiums paid, or in certain cases a cash surrender value.

Other important measures passed included the **Dangerous Drugs and Poisons (Amendment) Act**, 1923, which provided for the more efficient regulation of the sale of drugs, and the **Cotton Industry Act**, 1923, which enabled contributions to be made by cotton-spinners in Great Britain to the Empire Cotton Growing Corporation for the promotion of cotton growing. These contributions were continued and amended under the Acts of 1933 and 1938.

1924

The result of the General Election of 1923 gave the Conservatives 238 seats, the Socialists 191 and the Liberals 158. So that although the Conservatives were still the largest party, the Socialists and Liberals were able to outvote them. When Parliament met on 21st January 1924, a Socialist vote of 'No Confidence' was carried by 328 votes to 256 with 138 Liberals voting with the Socialists to defeat the Conservative government. Mr Baldwin immediately resigned and the Socialist leader, Mr Ramsay MacDonald, formed the first Socialist administration in British history.

The main controversy during the election centred on unemployment policy. In their election manifesto, the Socialists had declared that 'the Labour Party alone had a positive remedy' yet when challenged in the House of Commons on 10th March 1924 to produce this positive remedy, Mr Tom Shaw, the Socialist Minister of Labour, stated: 'Does anybody think that we can produce schemes like rabbits out of our hats'.

The **Housing Act** of 1924, known as the Wheatley Act, provided for greatly increased subsidies. This measure, however, was not very successful, especially when compared with the Chamberlain Act.

Towards the end of July of that year the *Workmen's Weekly*, the official organ of the Communist Party, edited by Mr J. R. Campbell, published an 'Open Letter to the Fighting Forces' in which open sedition was advocated. This letter read:

'Form committees in every barracks, aerodrome and ship. Let this be the nucleus of an organisation that will prepare the whole of the soldiers, sailors, and airmen not merely to refuse to go to war, or to refuse to shoot strikers during industrial conflicts, but will make it possible for the workers, peasants and soldiers and airmen to go forward in a common attack upon the capitalists and smash capitalism for ever and institute the reign of the whole working class'.

Mr J. R. Campbell was arrested but, when he appeared at Bow Street, counsel for the Director of Public Prosecutions said that his instructions were to offer no evidence with the result that Campbell was discharged. What happened was that prosecution was very properly instituted but as a result of political pressure being brought on the government from within their own Party the charge was dropped.

Eventually the government were defeated on a motion demanding an inquiry into the Campbell case and at the Election which followed the Conservative Party under Mr Baldwin obtained a large majority.

1925

In every department of social legislation the Conservative government of 1925-1929 has to its credit a substantial record of achievement. Much of this was due to the Minister of Health, Mr Neville Chamberlain.

One of the outstanding measures passed by this administration was the **Widows' and Orphans' and Old Age Pensions Act,** 1925, which will always be associated with the names of Mr Winston Churchill and Mr Neville Chamberlain. This scheme, which was interlocked with health insurance, provided, free from any means test, the following benefits:

(a) Old age pensions of 10s (50p) a week to insured persons at 65, and pensions of the same amount to wives of qualified insured persons when they also reach 65.

(b) Pensions of 10s (50p) a week for widows of insured persons with additional allowances for dependent children up to the age of 14, or 16 if they remain at school.

(c) Orphans' pensions of 7s 6d (37½p) a week up to the age of 14, or 16 if remaining at school.

In introducing this measure to Parliament, Mr Chamberlain expressed in one brief sentence, the Conservative conception of the

State. He declared: 'Our policy is to use the great resources of the State, not for the distribution of an indiscriminate largesse, but to help those who have the will and desire to raise themselves to higher and better things'.

Also in 1925 an important **Public Health Act** was passed, which embodied many provisions which experience had shown to be useful to local authorities and gave them a wide range of powers to deal with matters of health.

During its period of office Mr Baldwin's Ministry set about improving the position of women and children. The first of these measures, the **Guardianship of Infants Act**, 1925, gave mothers equal rights with fathers in applying to the Courts as regards the custody, upbringing and administration of persons under 21.

The **Administration of Estates Act**, 1925, gave wives equal rights with husbands to inherit property if either dies intestate and the **Separation and Maintenance Act** of the same year safeguarded the position of women desiring separation orders and provided that the interest of the children should always come first.

Improved conditions for seamen were established under the **Merchant Shipping (International Labour Convention) Act**, 1925.

Of special importance to women was the establishment in 1925 of a permanent Food Council to prevent profiteering in food prices.

Unemployment was one of the major problems during the inter-war period and it is significant that it invariably increased rapidly under a Socialist government. Industry was assisted by the re-imposition of duties on imported motor-cars and parts, musical instruments, clocks and watches, which had been abolished by the previous Socialist administration. In addition an Act was passed giving a subsidy to home-grown sugar-beet. As a result, additional employment and wages were found for many thousands of agricultural workers. The success of these efforts can be judged by the fact that between November 1924, and April 1926, just before the General Strike, unemployment dropped from 1,228,023, the figure it had reached after eight months of Socialist rule, to 981,877. The General Strike, which was largely the result of Socialist agitation for political ends, brought considerable distress to the workers and cost the country about £400m. and unemployment rose to 1,612,700 by May 1926. By June 1929, it had dropped again to 1,100,125.

1926

Although this year was clouded by the General Strike, some useful measures were passed.

The **Education Act**, 1926, inaugurated the comprehensive scheme of reorganising the schools on different age groups on the basis of the report of the Consultative Committee of the Board of Education presided over by Sir Henry Hadow and known as the Hadow Report.

Workers employed in the paint trade were protected against lead poisoning by the **Lead Paint (Protection Against Poisoning) Act,** 1926.

The **Mining Industry Act,** 1926, provided for a 5 per cent levy on royalties to assist in the establishment of pithead baths.

A **Rural Housing Act** was passed enabling rural cottages to be improved and enlarged with favourable conditions for owners and tenants. The **Small Holdings and Allotments Act** provided greater facilities for the obtaining of small holdings and cottage holdings for owner-occupiers and tenants.

The **Midwives and Maternity Homes Act** provided for the registration and inspection of all maternity homes and prevented unqualified persons from attending women in childbirth.

In addition, under the **Legitimacy Act** of this year a child born out of wedlock could be legitimised by the subsequent marriage of its parents. Special provision was made for the rights of such children and they were enabled to inherit certain kinds of property. The **Adoption of Children Act** legalised and provided safeguards for adoption in certain cases approved by the Court.

An **Electricity Act** was passed to reorganize the whole system of electric supply. This measure established the Central Electricity Board and led to the construction of the grid system.

In addition a measure was passed dealing with the abatement of smoke nuisance.

A further step was taken to preserve the purity of milk by the **Milk and Dairies Order,** 1926, which included provisions for the registration of all dairies and charged local authorities with the duty of inspecting all cattle in dairy farms and of seeing that milk was produced and handled under clean conditions. The **Tuberculosis Order** provided for the notification and the slaughter, with compensation, of dangerously tuberculous cattle.

This year also saw the setting up of the British Broadcasting Corporation.

1927

As a sequel to the General Strike, the **Trade Disputes and Trade Unions Act,** 1927, was passed with the aim of preventing the trade unions from being used as instruments for the coercion of the State and to safeguard the rights and liberties of individual trade unionists. This measure provided that:

(*a*) General Strikes and general lock-outs were illegal and no man was to be penalised for refusing to take part in one.

(b) Intimidation was illegal, and no man was to be compelled by threats to cease work against his will.

(c) No member of a trade union was to be compelled to subscribe to the funds of a political party unless he expressed a desire to do so.

This measure did nothing to prevent strikes for industrial purposes, nor sympathetic strikes which were merely intended to bring pressure to bear upon an employer. Its main purpose was to put an end to strikes which aimed at the coercion of a popularly elected government of the intimidation of the community as a whole.

Yet another instance of the importance attached by this government to the right treatment of children was shown by the **Mental Deficiency Act** passed in 1927. This measure placed under care and treatment cases which arose after attacks of sleepy sickness. Formerly children so affected could not be dealt with unless certified as lunatics, and the Act altered the definition of mental deficiency so that they could now be treated without this certification. It also enabled cases to be classified and ensured that the best method of treatment would be adopted in each individual case.

For the protection of the sick, the Government passed in 1927 the **Nursing Homes Registration Act.** There was urgent need for the registration and supervision by the local authorities of nursing and maternity homes, especially those used by poorer persons. The effect of this Act was to improve the care and treatment of the sick and to ensure that they were attended by qualified nurses.

The **Unemployment Insurance Act,** 1927, placed the unemployment insurance scheme on an improved basis, made benefit a right, subject to the fulfilment of simple and reasonable conditions, and made special concessions in favour of disabled ex-Service men and in cases of illness. This Act did away with any question of 'dole'. The main principles of the Act, which were based on the unanimous findings of the committee appointed in 1925 under the chairmanship of Lord Blanesburgh, a committee which included the well-known Socialist, Miss Margaret Bondfield, were as follows:

(a) That there should be only one kind of benefit and that all insured persons should have a right to that benefit provided they fulfilled the statutory conditions.

(b) 'Extended' benefit, given at the Minister's discretion, should become a thing of the past.

(c) That proof of the claimant having a limited number of contributions within the past two years should be the main statutory condition.

(d) That heads of households should receive increased benefits.

(e) That young persons between 18 and 20 should pay reduced contributions and receive reduced benefits.

(f) That contributions should be reduced when the fund was out of debt.

(g) That there should be a simple and uniform system of deciding on claims.

In addition provision was made for courses of instruction in useful trades for young persons of 16 to 18 years of age. Up to April 1928, one hundred juvenile employment centres for boys and girls had been established in the areas of 43 local educational authorities. In addition a National Advisory Council for Juvenile Employment was set up to advise on the question of assisting young persons to enter suitable employment.

The **Landlord and Tenant Act,** 1927, was specially designed to protect the interests of the small shopkeeper. Its three main provisions were:

(a) The payment of compensation to the tenant at the expiry of his lease in respect of any improvements which he had effected.

(b) The payment of compensation for goodwill at the expiry of a tenant's lease.

(c) The tenant was given the right of appeal in all these matters to an independent tribunal and in certain cases a new lease could be granted by the tribunal.

Sir W. Perring, then President of the London Suburban Traders' Federation and a past President of the National Chamber of Trade, paid this tribute to the Act: 'I desire, on behalf of the retail traders of the country for whom I speak, to express our great thanks for this Bill'.

An important measure was passed in 1927 for the assistance of British films. At the Imperial Conference in 1926 it was agreed to be of the greatest importance that a large and increasing proportion of films exhibited throughout the Empire should be of Empire production. The **Cinematograph Films Act,** which was passed to secure this aim, gave a powerful impetus to the British film industry.

1928

An Act of great importance to the agricultural industry was the **Agricultural Credits Act,** 1928, which established a system of long-term and short-term credits for farmers. The **Agricultural Produce**

(**Grading and Marketing**) **Act** of the same year assisted the marketing of home agricultural produce by establishing better standards of grading and packing.

The **Shops (Hours of Closing) Act,** 1928, established a uniform closing hour for shops throughout the country, and extended the permitted hours for sale of chocolate and confectionery. It also abolished many restrictions which still survived the war regarding the sale of these and other articles in theatres, licensed premises, places of entertainment and shops.

The **Industrial and Provident Societies Act,** 1928, protected members of co-operative and other societies from having the liabilities on their shares increased without their written consent.

The **National Health Insurance Act,** 1928, provided greatly extended and improved health insurance benefits for all classes and swept away many restrictions which formerly gave rise to hardship. This measure provided that no person genuinely seeking work was to be penalised in respect of arrears of health insurance contributions. It is estimated that this concession benefited 2,500,000 insured persons. In addition it safeguarded the pensions rights of contributors of the age of 60 who had been continuously insured for ten years and then found themselves unemployed. Further it added new classes of workers to the combined health and pensions scheme, such as sub-contractors in building and other trades, contractors for stone-breaking, and other road work, hedgers, ditchers, thatchers, drainers and others engaged in similar agricultural work, market porters, bill-posters, shop window cleaners, cattle drovers, slaughterers and shore fishermen.

The **Equal Franchise Act,** 1928, completed a century of electoral reform by giving women the vote on the same terms as men at the age of 21 thus adding a further 5,250,000 to the electorate.

Miss Eleanor Rathbone, presiding at a meeting of the National Union of Societies for Equal Citizenship, in March 1929, said that it was to the Conservative government that they 'owed the achievement of the cause which they had set before them for so long'.

1929

The **Local Government Act,** 1929, combined the previous Poor Law health services with the existing local government administration and so ensured under larger administrative units better and more efficient health services, institutions and mental treatment.

Realising that the revival of industry and agriculture was being seriously handicapped by the heavy burden of local rates and high transport charges, the government, in 1929, decided to relieve all productive industries of three-quarters of their rates, to free agricultural land and farm buildings entirely from rates and to relieve railways, docks and harbours from three-quarters of the rates on the condition that this waiving was passed on in the form of reduced freights on certain classes of materials and goods.

The bulk of this rating relief went to the basic industries in parts of the country where unemployment was then heaviest.

This help to industry was not granted at the expense of other ratepayers because local authorities were more than compensated for the loss of these rates by increased State Grants (the Block Grant). This Block Grant was distributed on a formula basis which ensured that the greater amount of the additional assistance went to the most needy districts.

The General Election, which took place in May 1929, resulted in the return of 260 Conservatives, 288 Socialists, 59 Liberals and 8 Independents. Accordingly on 5th June 1929, Mr Ramsay MacDonald formed his second Socialist administration.

The two and a quarter years of Socialist administration from 1929–1931 proved to be one of the most disastrous periods in the history of the country. The outstanding features were a calamitous decline in British trade, a rise in unemployment to close on three millions, and a reckless and improvident financial policy. In the autumn of 1929 an economic and financial crisis swept the United States and spread to this country, the economic stability of which had already been considerably weakened by the policy of the government. The Socialist administration failed to deal with the crisis and was replaced in August 1931, by the National government, Mr Ramsay MacDonald remaining as Prime Minister.

1931

The period 1931 to 1939 may be divided into two parts, the first part up to 1935 was one of economic and financial recovery and rising prosperity. The second period, however, from 1935 to 1939, was one of growing international tension, which culminated in the outbreak of war in September 1939.

The government had to take immediate steps to remedy both the financial and the trade position. One of the principal features of the new government's financial policy was the conversion of the National Debt and the general lowering of interest rates. The Bank Rate was maintained as low as 2 per cent from 1932 onwards. This 'cheap money' policy effected an annual reduction to taxpayers of some £70m. In addition the Unemployment Fund which in 1931 had a debt of over £100m. and was incurring further debt at the rate of £1m. a week, was placed in a solvent position. Again during the period 1931–1939 the total savings of the people increased by over £1,000m.

1932

Trade recovery was greatly assisted by the introduction of the general tariff under the **Abnormal Importations Act,** 1931, the **Import Duties Act,** 1932, and the **Ottawa Agreements Act,** 1932. The Import Duties Act, which laid the foundations upon which the British tariff is built, imposed, as from March 1932, a general *ad valorem* customs duty of 10 per cent on all imports into the United Kingdom other than certain specified goods and goods imported from the Dominions and Colonies.

The Abnormal Importations Act imposed an *ad valorem* duty of 50 per cent on a large number of foreign manufactured goods where it was proved that quantities far in excess of normal requirements were being imported.

The Imperial Economic Conference held at Ottawa in July and August 1932, marked an important stage in the government's tariff policy. At the conference agreements were arrived at between the representatives of the United Kingdom and the Dominions and India and Southern Rhodesia under which, the United Kingdom, gave free entry for Dominion goods imported into the United Kingdom. The free entry was limited, however, by certain reservations in respect of eggs, poultry, butter, cheese and other milk products. The conclusion of these agreements, which led to the resignation of Sir Herbert Samuel and certain other Liberal Ministers, undoubtedly contributed in great measure to our trade recovery. Our balance of trade was restored from a deficit of £104m. in 1931 to a surplus of £33m. in 1935.

The **Wheat Act,** 1932, was of great benefit to agriculture. This measure established a quota scheme to secure for the home farmer an increased price for all home-grown wheat of millable quality, and to give him, in addition, a secure market for his wheat. The money required to finance this scheme did not come from either the taxpayer or the government but was provided by the flour millers and flour importers who made 'quota payments' into the Wheat Fund, which was administered by the Wheat Commission set up under the Act.

During the eight years of the National Government outstanding progress was made in the development of our social services. Improvements and extensions took place in practically every branch and in 1939 the British system of social services was more far-reaching and comprehensive than any other country in the world. This was acknowledged by Mr George Tomlinson, a prominent member of the Socialist Party, who in the course of a speech on 12th May 1944, declared: 'In Social Security we are in front of the world. We mean to stay in front of the world.'

Two important measures in the field of social reform were passed in 1932. The **Transitional Payments (Determination of Need) Act** made important concessions to persons requiring Public Assistance.

The **Children and Young Persons Act** amended the treatment of juvenile offenders. Special juvenile courts were created. In addition the age of criminal liability for the death sentence was raised. A further provision of this Act was for the amalgamation of reformatories and industrial schools into approved schools. New restrictions on the employment of children under twelve were also imposed.

1933

Housing progress reached hitherto unparalleled proportions while the National Government was in office. Out of the 4,200,000 houses built during the inter-war period, some 2,400,000 were erected during the period 1931 to 1939 and it is significant that private enterprise was responsible for three out of every four houses built. The rate of building at the peak was 346,000 a year as compared with an average of less than 200,000 for the two years 1930–1931.

The first stage in the government's housing programme was to create the conditions which would enable the building industry to perform its proper function of providing the normal housing requirements of the people. The **Housing (Financial Provisions) Act,** 1933, was accordingly passed which rectified the position as between the private builder and local authorities under the 1924 Act.

In this way private builders were able to meet the general needs of housing without state assistance and local anthorities were able to concentrate on subsidy building for the campaign against slums and overcrowding. The success of this policy can be judged from the fact that during the six years 1933–1938 about 1,500,000 slum dwellers were rehoused; by 1939 the proportion of people still living in unfit or overcrowded houses had been reduced to some 6 per cent and in the months immediately before the outbreak of war in 1939 the rate of rehousing in the slums reached 1,000 a day.

Another important measure was the **Children and Young Persons Act** of this year, which gave additional power to local authorities to regulate by by-laws the conditions, number of hours per day and week and the times at which children of fourteen may be employed, the intervals to be allowed for meals and rest, and the holidays to be granted.

The **Agriculture Marketing Act,** 1933, made provision for the registration by order of the imports of any agricultural product into the United Kingdom when producers of the product concerned had shown their intention of adopting internal marketing. By 1934, schemes for hops, pigs and bacon, milk and potatoes were in operation covering about one-third of the total value of home agricultural produce. A second **Marketing Act,** 1933, gave power to a Marketing Board to pay compensation to their producers in respect of losses, and also to grant loans.

The **Road and Rail Traffic Act,** 1933, made provision for regulating the carriage of goods on roads by motor vehicles. This measure also set up a Transport Advisory Council for the purpose of giving advice and assistance to the Minister of Transport in connection with means and facilities for transport and its co-ordination.

The **London Passenger Transport Act,** 1933, provided for the establishment of the London Passenger Transport Board and for the transfer to the Board of all transport undertakings operating within what was termed, under the Act, the London Passenger Transport Area.

1934

The **Road Traffic Act,** 1934, was mainly concerned with safety on the roads and introduced among other provisions, the 30 miles-per-hour speed limit in built-up areas.

In April 1934, the Government caused urgent enquiries to be made into unemployment in typical places in Durham, South Wales, Cumberland and Scotland. The reports of these investigations were published early in November and before the end of the year the **Special Areas (Development and Improvement) Act** had been passed to bring about improved economic conditions in these areas. By 1939 over 2,500,000 more people were employed than in 1931 and industrial production was nearly doubled. Wages rose to the highest level since 1922 and retail trade increased by more than 25 per cent.

An outstanding measure of reform in the field of unemployment insurance was the **Unemployment Act,** 1934. This measure restored the benefit cuts made during the emergency of 1931 and covered 75 per cent of all unemployment by insurance. In addition, unemployment allowances on a national basis were provided by the Unemployment Assistance Board, established under this Act, to make provisions for the needs of the able-bodied unemployed who could not qualify for insurance benefits and who, in the past, had recourse to the Poor Law for assistance. The Act also made improvements in the rates of children's allowances payable to those in receipt of unemployment insurance benefit.

The **Shop Act,** 1934, which covered some 400,000 shop assistants, regulated the hours of employment in retail and wholesale shops of young persons under 18 and laid down regulations as to sanitary and other arrangements.

Under the **Milk Act** the Government provided direct financial assistance to the milk industry and started milk in schools.

The important **Workmen's Compensation (Coal Mines) Act,** 1934, provided that owners of coal mines must insure against, or otherwise ensure the discharge of their liabilities to pay workmen's compensation under previous Workmen's Compensation Acts. This was one of the few cases of a private member's bill reaching the statute book; it was introduced by Mr Godfrey Nicholson, Conservative MP for Morpeth.

1935

In the autumn of 1935, the National Government successfully appealed to the electorate for a fresh mandate.

An improvement in the industrial position enabled the government to pass in 1935 the **National Health Insurance and Contributory Pensions Act,** which brought a new element of security into the lives of the 18m. insured persons under the scheme by safeguarding full pension rights and medical, maternity and additional treatment rights without further contributions for sick and unemployed persons with ten years' current insurances at the time of ceasing work. In addition, contribution arrears due to proved unemployment were completely excused. Mr T. W. Huntley, President of the National Association of Insurance Committees of England, described this Act as a boon and a blessing.

The **Housing Act,** 1935, gave further impetus to the abatement of overcrowding by providing special Exchequer subsidies.

1936

The **Agriculture Act** of this year began a special unemployment insurance scheme for agriculture and thereby benefited some 720,000 agricultural workers.

The **Midwives Act,** 1936, required local authorities to establish adequate services of salaried and trained midwives. In this way a national service of midwives was set up to promote safer motherhood. The infant mortality rate in England and Wales decreased from 66 per 1,000 births in 1931 to 50 in 1939, and the maternal mortality rate from 3.95 per 1,000 births in 1931 to 2.82 in 1939.

In the field of education more and better schools were being provided, the size of classes was being reduced and the school meals and medical services considerably extended.

By the Milk in School scheme, inaugurated in 1934, about 2,500,000 school children were receiving a daily ration of milk while over 500,000 necessitous children received it free.

The **Education Act,** 1936, made provision for the raising of the school-leaving age from fourteen to fifteen from 1st September 1939, but owing to the outbreak of war this was prevented from being carried out.

On 27th May of this year the *Queen Mary* made her maiden voyage. This liner was completed on Clydebank by the Cunard White Star Company which received certain loans from the Treasury for the purpose.

The *Queen Elizabeth* was being built at Clydebank when war broke out and made her maiden voyage in peace time on 25th October 1946.

1937

In May 1937, Mr Neville Chamberlain succeeded Mr Baldwin as Prime Minister. It is one of the ironies of history that, having achieved so much in the field of social reform and being admirably equipped to lead this country along the path of prosperity and social security, the three years of Mr Chamberlain's premiership were spent under the shadow of an international conflict.

In the field of social reform, 1937 saw the passing of the first comprehensive measure dealing with factory conditions for over thirty years. The **Factories Act,** 1937, improved the working conditions of some 7,000,000 workers employed in factories and workshops. Under this measure a limit of 48 hours per week was imposed on the working hours of women and young persons, with special regulations regarding accidents, cleanliness, ventilation, lighting, etc.

The **Voluntary Pensions Act,** 1937, gave an opportunity to men and women of limited means, who were outside the scope of compulsory insurance, to contribute on a voluntary basis for old-age pensions and widow's and orphan's pensions. The **National Health Insurance (Juvenile Contributors and Young Persons) Act** made medical treatment available to juveniles immediately on entering insurable employment instead of requiring them to wait until the full health insurance age of 16. About one million juveniles benefited from this measure.

In order to assist in improving the physical fitness of the nation, the **Physical Training and Recreation Act** was passed to enable grants to be made for the provision of gymnasia and equipment and for other recreation facilities. In this way a Service of Youth scheme came into being.

Two important measures were passed in 1937 dealing with agriculture. The **Agriculture Act** of that year, which was designed to increase the fertility and productivity of both land and stock, rendered possible a quick adaptation of the agricultural industry to wartime conditions. It provided for Exchequer contributions towards the cost of lime and basic slag, drainage schemes, stamping out animal disease, and towards prices received for wheat, barley and oats.

The **Livestock Industry Act,** 1937, provided up to £5m. per annum to subsidise the home producers of fat cattle.

Later, in May 1939, a government grant of £2 an acre towards the cost of ploughing up grassland was made.

1938

In spite of the gathering war clouds, 1938 produced a very fruitful crop of legislation. The **Housing (Financial Provisions) Act** made possible, for the first time, the large-scale building of new houses for agricultural workers. A **Rent Restriction Act** was passed, bringing the rentals of over four million of the smaller type of house property under control, and the **Equalisation of Subsidies Housing (Financial Provisions) Act** brought subsidies for slums and overcrowding to the same level to enable both problems to be tackled with equal vigour.

Two important measures were passed dealing with the care of young persons. The **Children and Young Persons Act,** 1938, extended the powers of Courts of Summary Jurisdiction in regard to the problem of the protection, custody, supervision and care of children and young persons. The **Young Persons (Employment) Act** improved conditions in regard to overtime and intervals for meals and secured weekly holidays for young persons under eighteen in many occupations.

The **Holidays With Pay Act,** 1938, enabled Trade Boards, Agricultural Wages Committees and the Road Haulage Central Wages Board to provide holidays with pay in addition to fixing wage rates. This Act was intended as an advance step to legislation covering all workers and by 1939 some ten million people were receiving holidays with pay under these arrangements.

The **Poor Law (Amendment) Act,** 1938, permitted a small weekly allowance to be paid to persons aged 65 and over, who were inmates of Poor Law Institutions.

The **Blind Persons Act** enabled the blind to qualify for non-contributory old age pensions at 40 years of age instead of 50.

The **Hire Purchase Act,** 1938, gave protection against abuses in respect of hire purchase and the sale of goods on credit.

In the coal industry, the **Mining Royalties Act,** 1938, brought about the state acquisition of coal royalties.

The **Workmen's Compensation (Amendment) Act,** passed in 1938, covered persons engaged in plying for hire with any vehicle or vessel. In June 1938, a royal commission was set up under the chairmanship of Sir Hector Hetherington to inquire into the whole system of workmen's compensation, but its sittings were suspended owing to the war.

1939

Although home affairs were well in the background during 1939, some important measures were passed. The **Unemployment Insurance Act,** 1939, clarified the position of insured persons on recognised holidays and provided easier conditions under which separate periods of unemployment might count as one for benefit purposes.

The **Cotton Industry (Reorganisation) Act** of this year set up a Cotton Industry Board with certain powers and functions for securing the better organisation of the industry, a representative council of the industry to advise the Board and an independent cotton industry advisory committee to assist the Board of Trade in matters relating to the industry. Among the powers conferred on the Cotton Industry Board was the power to conduct market research and investigation.

The **Adoption of Children (Regulation) Act** provided safeguards for the adoption of children and the **Cancer Act** improved the facilities for the treatment of persons suffering from cancer.

1940–1945
The four-year plan

IN SPITE OF THE WAR considerable progress was made in the field of social reform during the years 1940–1945 under the National and Coalition Governments, in which the Conservatives were in a majority.

1940

Among the most remarkable achievements during the years of war were the many improvements which were effected in the realm of old age pensions; in fact, no less than four major Acts were passed. The first of these measures, the **Old Age and Widows' Pension Act,** 1940, lowered the pensionable age for insured women from sixty-five to sixty, as a result of which some three million women secured direct benefit. This Act also started a supplementary pensions scheme for old age and widow pensioners in need. The supplementary pensions were paid at the entire cost of the State, and were received as a statutory right providing the cases complied with the Assistance Board's regulations.

The **Unemployment Insurance Act,** 1940, substantially increased the rates of unemployment benefit and extended the unemployment insurance scheme to 'black-coated' workers earning below certain limits.

Several Acts were passed during the war dealing with Workmen's Compensation. The **Workmen's Compensation (Supplementary Allowances) Act,** 1940, relieved hardship for the families of workmen injured in industrial accidents by providing weekly allowances to supplement their compensation payments.

In addition, the **Workmen's Compensation and Benefit (Byssinosis) Act** of the same year covered the victims of the respiratory disease, known as byssinosis, which was prevalent amongst men employed in dusty parts of the cotton mills, especially in card and blowing rooms.

The **Agricultural Wages (Regulation) Amendment Act,** 1940, was of benefit to agricultural workers in that it enabled a national minimum wage standard to be fixed.

Nutritional facilities were an important part of the Coalition Government's food policy, the success of which was proved by the fact that the health of the nation was maintained throughout the war.

Under the national milk scheme introduced in 1940, milk was supplied to expectant mothers and all children under five; of the three and a half million mothers and children who benefited, about one-third were entitled to free milk, the rest receiving it at reduced prices. In addition the Milk-in-Schools scheme provided a further four million children with free or cheap milk. Fruit juices and cod-liver oil were made available to expectant mothers and to children under five. Two million children received meals in grant-aided schools at a low price.

As a result of the large number of people engaged in various kinds of war work there was an urgent need to extend catering facilities and by 1943 there were 10,000 canteens for workers in factories and mines and over 2,000 British Restaurants for the public as a whole.

1941

The second of the four major war-time measures dealing with old age pensions was the **Determination of Needs Act**, 1941. By abolishing the Household Means Test and substituting a test of personal need, this Act brought about an important reform in the method of administering old age pensions and so helped 200,000 more pensioners. Experience of the 1940 Act had shown that while in many cases it had achieved beneficial results there were a large number of instances where it involved humiliations to pensioners in its application to members of the household. One of its drawbacks had been that in order to assess the amount of the supplementary pension a complicated assessment was made of the wages and resources of members of the household. The underlying principle of the new scheme was that no applicant without resources of his own would be left dependent on other members of the household for means to buy clothing and other necessary personal requirements.

The **National Health Insurance, Contributory Pensions and Workmen's Compensation Act**, 1941, increased the weekly rates of sickness and disablement benefits and raised the annual income limits for Unemployment and Health Insurance from £350 to £420. This measure also brought within the scope of the workmen's compensation scheme non-manual workers who were remunerated at a yearly rate between £350, the former limit, and £420.

1942

In July 1942, Parliament approved a number of regulations increasing the scale rates of supplementary pensions. The cost of these regulations amounted to about £12m. a year.

1943

The **Determination of Needs Act,** 1943, applied the principles of the 1941 Act to Public Assistance and thus carried a stage further the break-up of the Poor Law. Widowed pensioners under the age of sixty who had children to support became eligible for supplementary pensions in addition to their widow's and children's allowances, if any. Moreover, under this Act, a widow in receipt of the supplementary pension was entitled to continue to receive it after the last child had reached the age of sixteen and she was, therefore, no longer eligible to secure a children's allowance. In addition this measure instituted a number of improvements in the system of calculating the resources of applicants.

Two measures dealing with Workmen's Compensation were passed during 1943. The **Workmen's Compensation (Temporary Increases) Act** provided for increases in the compensation rates and the **Workmen's Compensation Act** included for compensation purposes workers suffering from any form of pneumoconiosis, i.e., fibrosis of the lungs due to silica dust, asbestos dust, or other dust, and also the condition of the lungs known as dustreculation. Provision was also made to cover workmen employed in coal mining totally disabled by pneumoconiosis who had not been entitled to benefit under previous Acts. In addition provision was made for the re-calculation of compensation where the standard rate of pay in the industry was increased after the accident.

The **Catering Wages Act,** 1943, established a statutory commission to deal with the remuneration and conditions of employment in the catering trades, with power to recommend the establishment of Wage Boards, where existing arrangements were inadequate. This Act recognised the importance of attracting tourists to this country after the war and in addition to their powers regarding wages and conditions in the catering trades, the commission was empowered to make any inquiries they thought fit to meet the requirements of the public, including in particular the requirements of visitors from overseas and for developing the tourist traffic.

The **Nurses Act** of 1943 was of immense benefit to the nursing profession. As a result of this measure, which was based on the First Report of the Rushcliffe Committee on Nurses' Salaries, national salary scales were adopted throughout the nursing profession, and the great majority of nurses received increased salaries.

On 21st March 1943, Mr Winston Churchill made his memorable broadcast in which he outlined a Four-Year Plan for this country after the war. This plan was to consist of five or six measures including a scheme to provide a high level of employment, a comprehensive system of national insurance covering the whole population, the recasting of our educational system and a comprehensive National Health Service.

1944

In March 1944, the Coalition Government published proposals for a National Health Service, which would bring the benefits of every type of medical service to the population as a whole. The Coalition scheme was based on the traditional, personal, confidential relationship of people with doctors of their own choice and not in any sense upon an impersonal relationship with some bureaucratic service. The principles of this scheme were accepted by Parliament and Mr H. U. Willink, the Conservative Minister of Health, immediately initiated discussions with representatives of the medical profession and other interested bodies as to the best means of translating the new proposals into legislative form. These discussions were nearing agreement when the General Election intervened.

The Service eventually started to operate in July 1948 following considerable controversy between the Socialist government and the medical profession. The doctors feared that the ultimate aim of the Socialist government was to create a full-time state salaried medical service and that this aim might be achieved under the National Health Service Act 1946 which brought the Service into being. However, as a result of the pressure from the medical profession, which was supported by Conservatives, the National Health Service (Amendment) Act 1949 was passed which made it clear that a full-time state salaried medical service could not be brought into being without fresh legislation. It is interesting that the 1946 Act provided specifically under Section 5 for pay beds in Health Service hospitals which were intended for use by private fee-paying patients. Mr Aneurin Bevan, the Minister of Health at the time, justified the provision of pay beds within the Hospital Service on these grounds: 'If we do not permit fees in hospitals, we will lose many specialists from the public hospitals, for they will go to nursing homes. . . . We want to keep our specialists attached to our hospitals and not send them into nursing homes. Behind this there is a principle of some importance. If the State owned a theatre it would not charge the same prices for the different seats.' (*Hansard*, 30th April 1946)

In May 1944, the Government published its White Paper on Employment Policy. This White Paper, which emphasised that one of the primary aims and responsibilities of government was the maintenance of a high and stable level of employment after the war, contained proposals whereby government policy could be directed to achieving this aim, under a system which allowed the qualities of energy, skill and enterprise to have full play.

By 1944 the credit balance of the Unemployment Fund was £294m. on the general fund and over £8m. on the agricultural account; moreover, some 90 per cent of the employed population was covered by insurance.

In June 1941, the Government had made arrangements for a comprehensive survey of existing schemes of social insurance and allied services to be made by an inter-departmental committee under the chairmanship of Sir William (later Lord) Beveridge.

The famous Beveridge Report, which was published in 1942, affirmed that the British social security system was 'on a scale not surpassed and hardly rivalled in any other country of the world'.

In his broadcast of 21st March 1943, Mr Winston Churchill declared that we were now ready for another great advance in the field of social insurance and that a scheme for the extension of our present social insurance system should have a leading place in post-war reconstruction. Accordingly in September 1944, the Government published proposals for a comprehensive scheme of national insurance, including provisions for family allowances. This scheme, which, broadly speaking, followed the lines of the Beveridge Report, was to be unified in administration and include the whole population, taking account of the varying ways of life and requirements of the different sections of the community. The chief features of this plan, which formed the basis of the Socialist government's National Insurance Act, 1946, were increased pension rates and improved sickness and unemployment benefit. Provision was also made for a death grant. An integral part of the Coalition scheme was the industrial injury insurance scheme. Henceforth, workmen's compensation was to be treated not as part of the law of employer's liability but as a social service, comprehensive in scope and covering, broadly speaking, all persons working under a contract of service or apprenticeship, except those under school-leaving age.

The **Ministry of National Insurance Act,** 1944, was the first measure to implement the new national insurance scheme and provided for the appointment of a Minister of National Insurance and for the transfer to him, with certain exceptions, of responsibility for the existing social services. The Labour government's 1946 legislation, providing for comprehensive schemes of National Insurance and Industrial Injuries, started to operate in July 1948.

In his Four-Year Plan speech Mr Winston Churchill had outlined the broad purpose of education and the general form which it should take after the war. He defined the broad purpose of education in the following words:

'The future of the world is to the highly educated races, who alone can handle the scientific apparatus necessary for pre-eminence in peace or survival in war.

'We must beware of trying to build a society in which nobody counts for anything except a politician or an official, a society where enterprise gains no reward and thrift no privileges. Human beings are endowed with infinitely varying qualities and dispositions and each one is different from the other. We cannot make them all the same. It would be a pretty dull world if we did. It is in our power, however, to secure equal opportunities for all. The facilities for advanced education must be evened out and multiplied, no one who can take advantage of a higher education should be denied his chance.' (Broadcast speech, 21st March 1943)

The **Education Act,** 1944, which will always be associated with the name of Mr R. A. (later Lord) Butler the Conservative Minister of Education in the Coalition Government, was generally acknowledged to be an outstanding measure of educational progress and the great bulk of it came into effect from 1st April 1945. Its principal reforms included:

(*a*) Total provision for the raising of the school-leaving age to fifteen, without exceptions, from a date not later than 1st April 1947, with a further raising to sixteen as soon as practicable;

(*b*) the abolition of tuition fees in all schools maintained by local education authorities (this provision came into effect from 1st April 1945);

(*c*) provision of more nursery schools for children under five;

(*d*) the complete reorganisation of public elementary schools;

(*e*) increased grants for non-provided schools; and

(*f*) a clear recognition of the place of religion in school life.

Two central advisory committees were established under the Act to advise the Minister on matters connected with educational theory and practice.

In order to meet the need which would arise after the war for more teachers, the Coalition Government devised an emergency scheme to attract to the teaching profession men and women from the Forces and other forms of national service. In addition increased financial provision was made to meet the postwar requirements of the universities.

The immediate housing need after the war was estimated at some one million houses, a figure which represented roughly three years' output at the height of our building activity before the war.

Bearing in mind, however, the size of the available building force, the Government announced that the maximum target which could properly be adopted was one of 300,000 permanent houses by the end of the second year after the cessation of hostilities in Europe; together with some 200,000 temporary houses.

The first measure passed to facilitate the provision of houses after the war was the **Housing (Temporary Provisions) Act,** 1944, which made provision for housing needs by extending the Exchequer subsidy, granted under the 1938 Act, for slum clearance and abatement of overcrowding, to all permanent houses and flats provided by local authorities.

In July 1944, the Minister of Health announced that legislation would be introduced to make the Exchequer subsidy available for houses provided for general needs by private enterprise, subject to conditions as to size, construction, selling price and rent. The General Election, however, prevented the Coalition Government from carrying out this policy and, with the return of a Socialist government, housing policy was hostile to private enterprise building.

In regard to temporary accommodation, the **Housing (Temporary Accommodation) Act,** 1944, authorised expenditure up to £150m. on the provision of some 200,000 temporary houses, which were to be publicly owned and licensed. These temporary houses were essentially intended to be used for a limited number of years.

The housing needs of rural areas were not overlooked by the Coalition Government, which recognised the continued need for increased food production in this country; accordingly a measure was introduced to extend the period of operation of the **Housing (Rural Workers) Acts,** under which state-assisted reconditioning was carried out and to amend these Acts so as to bring them into line with current conditions and price levels. Again the General Election prevented further progress of this measure and it was scrapped by the new government. As a result of this decision all state-aided reconditioning of rural cottages ceased in October 1945, and many agricultural workers were condemned to living conditions far below what they need have been.

A number of steps were taken during 1944 to assist the resettlement of service men and women in civilian life after the war. The **Reinstatement in Civil Employment Act** made provision for the reinstatement of service men and women in their former civilian occupations and a scheme was devised to enable men and women to obtain, on demobilisation, the further education or training which their war service had interrupted. A training and resettlement scheme for disabled persons, whatever the cause of disablement, was instituted under the **Disabled Persons (Employment) Act,** 1944. Where training and employment under this measure could not be found for all disabled persons, the Minister of Labour was empowered to give preference to ex-service men and women. Up to 1945, over 40,000 people or 75 per cent of persons interviewed under this Act had entered training or employment.

Wartime difficulties facing agriculture were tackled by intense efforts to increase production and lessen our dependence on exports.

The anxieties of producers were removed by the policy of guaranteed markets and prices. As a result there was a 70 per cent increase in home food production and an increased area of one million acres under the plough.

Three measures were passed during 1944 for the permanent assistance of British agriculture. The **Agriculture (Miscellaneous Provisions) Act,** besides providing for the establishment of a National Advisory Service, grants for lime, water supplies to farms, and other matters, extended the financial assistance which could be granted to the English and Scottish Agricultural Corporations, which were thereby enabled to reduce their rate of interest on mortgage and improvement loans from $4\frac{1}{2}$ per cent to $3\frac{1}{2}$ per cent and to increase their loans to a total of £31.5m. instead of the previous total of £13m.

The **Food and Drugs (Milk and Dairies) Act** introduced a number of important reforms for the improvement of the quality of milk production in this country.

The **Rural Water Supplies and Sewerage Act,** 1944, made provision for the payment of Exchequer grants towards the expenses incurred by local authorities in providing water supplies in rural areas. In addition this measure laid down that it was the duty of a local authority to provide a piped water supply to every rural locality in its districts in which there were houses or schools.

The **Town and Country Planning Act,** 1944, provided a basis for town planning after the war. This measure empowered local planning authorities more simply and quickly to acquire all land essential to the rebuilding of reconstruction areas – namely areas which had suffered extensive war damage and areas of bad layout and obsolete development which needed to be treated as a whole. Provision was made in both cases for the acquisition of land lying outside the immediate limits of the areas concerned. In general, the purchase price of land compulsorily acquired by local authorities was to be the price current in March 1939, but an additional 30 per cent was to be paid to an owner-occupier.

Other important measures passed during 1944 were the **Pensions (Increase) Act,** 1944, which made improvements in certain ranges of state and local government pensions, and the **Unemployment Insurance (Increase of Benefit) Act** which increased weekly rates of unemployment benefit.

The **Herring Industry Act,** 1944, assisted the post-war revival of the herring industry by enabling grants up to a total of £820,000 over a period of five years to be made towards the provision of boats and equipment to herring fishermen and others wishing to engage in the industry. Apart from fishermen the persons to be helped included those who had served whole-time in the armed forces or the Mercantile Marine. Under the Act grants up to one-third of the total cost of the boat and equipment could be made.

The year 1944 saw important developments in the field of electoral reform. In February, the Coalition Government set up a conference on electoral reform and redistribution of seats under the Chairmanship of Mr Speaker (Colonel Clifton Brown). The main purpose of the **House of Commons (Redistribution of Seats) Act,** 1944, which was the first measure to give effect to certain recommendations of this conference, was to provide for the appointment of four permanent Boundary Commissions to arrange the distribution of seats, one each for England, Scotland, Wales and Northern Ireland. In this way Parliamentary representation is kept constantly under review by each commission, which submits periodical reports as to any changes that are considered necessary.

1945

The **Family Allowances Act,** 1945, implemented the provisions of the Coalition Government's national insurance scheme in regard to family allowances by providing for the payment from the Exchequer of an allowance at the weekly rate of 5s (25p) for each child of sixteen and under except the first or only child.

The Coalition Government's White Paper on Employment Policy was based on the realisation that during the war this country had been forced to sell the greater part of her overseas investments in order to pay for essential imports of food and raw materials and that, in order to maintain our standard of living after the war, we must continue to import from abroad a large proportion of foodstuffs and raw materials, which to a greater extent than ever before would have to be paid for by the export of goods and services. The White Paper recognised that the Government had an important part to play in facilitating the expansion of our export trade. Accordingly the **Export Guarantees Act,** 1945, made provision for the expansion of our overseas trade after the war by increasing from £75m. to £200m. the maximum liability which could be incurred at any time by the Board of Trade in respect of guarantees given against loss on export trade transactions.

The **Distribution of Industry Act,** 1945, implemented the proposal which was contained in the White Paper on Employment Policy to take definite measures to check the development of localised unemployment in particular areas and industries after the war. This measure was designed to enable the Government to secure a proper distribution of industry over the country as a whole by stimulating the industrial and social development of areas to be known as development areas in which there was a special danger of unemployment and by controlling further industrial development in other areas where such control would appear to be desirable for economic, social or strategic reasons.

The **Income Tax Act,** 1945, gave effect to the proposals for changes in the taxation of industry after the war recommended in the White Peper on Employment Policy and announced by the Chancellor of the Exchequer, Sir John Anderson, in his Budget speech of April 1944. Under this measure provision was made for helping post-war industry and agriculture by way of tax reliefs designed to assist the modernisation and re-equipment of buildings, plant and machinery.

Under the **Wages Councils Act,** which benefited some 15.5m. persons, provision was made for the continuation of the Trade Boards under the new title of Wages Councils and for the establishment of Wages Councils where voluntary machinery was inadequate and reasonable standards of remuneration were not being maintained. It is interesting to note that the Trade Board system was originally introduced by Mr Winston Churchill in 1909, a fact which was acknowledged by Mr Ernest Bevin, who paid the following tribute to Mr Churchill during the second reading of this measure on 16th January 1945.

> 'Perhaps I may deal for a moment with the history of the trade boards system. It was introduced in 1909 by the present Prime Minister. Of all the things he has done, I know of none better for the down-trodden masses of the country than the basic legislation then introduced.'

The **Water Act,** 1945, embodied proposals for a National Water Policy by placing upon the Minister of Health the statutory duty of promoting throughout England and Wales the provision of adequate water supplies and the conservation of water resources so that water was provided for all reasonable needs of householders, agriculture and industry. Provision was also made for a Central Advisory Water Committee to advise the government on general questions relating to water and for local joint advisory committees to meet the future needs of their areas.

The **Teachers' (Superannuation) Act,** 1945, brought the ruling definition of contributory service for pension purposes into conformity with the new educational system introduced by the Education Act of 1944. As a result, contributory service for pension purposes was extended to cover additonal teachers, mainly supplementary teachers not previously pensionable, as well as full-time youth leaders employed in grant-aided service, and some further classes of educational organisers employed by local education authorities or by grant-aided organisations.

Under the **Forestry Act,** which was intended to prepare for the post-war development of forestry, ministerial responsibility was secured for forestry policy and administration. The Forestry Commission was retained as a single continuing body responsible directly to the Ministers for carrying out all operations connected with forestry, including the training of foresters, research, and the management of forest holdings and generally for giving advice on forestry policy. The measure also transferred from the Commissioners to the Minister the power to acquire land, either by agreement or compulsorily.

The **Representation of the People Act,** 1945, carried out certain important electoral reforms in accordance with the report of the Speaker's Conference. This measure provided for the assimilation of the Parliamentary and local government franchises, the resumption of local government elections suspended during the war, and the publication of registers at certain fixed dates. This Act, which added some seven million electors to the local government roll, also made provisions for postal voting by service voters and war workers abroad.

PART TWO

Thirteen years of progress 1951 to 1964

A CONSERVATIVE GOVERNMENT was returned to office at the October 1951 General Election and this was the start of thirteen years of continuous progress and improvement in the conditions of the people under successive Conservative Prime Ministers – Sir Winston Churchill (October 1951–April 1955); Sir Anthony Eden (later Lord Avon) (April 1955–January 1957); Mr Harold Macmillan (January 1957–October 1963); Sir Alec Douglas-Home (now Lord Home) (October 1963–October 1964).

The inheritance of failure from Labour

The achievements of these thirteen years of Conservative government are all the more impressive when considered against the background of the legacy of failure inherited from the post-war Labour government under Mr (later Lord) Attlee which had come into office following the General Election of July 1945.

Sir Winston Churchill in a broadcast on 8th October 1951 summed up the reasons for Labour's failure in these words:

> 'The keeping on of the wartime controls and restrictions has hampered our recovery, fettered our enterprise and enormously added to the cost and apparatus of government. Here the difference between the two Parties may be thus summed up. Our opponents say: "The more controls and restrictions we have, the nearer we approach the Socialist ideal." The Conservatives say: "The fewer we have the better for a vigorous and expanding Britain." '

Some of the main results of Labour's policies are summarised briefly below:

Trade deficits

Throughout most of the Socialist period our overseas trade accounts failed to balance. In 1951, the deficit between our visible and invisible exports and our imports was running at the rate of nearly £400m. a year. Government-administered controls, permits, licences, quotas and allocations maintained a stranglehold on enterprise.

The country lurched from one crisis to another, and as Sir Stafford Cripps, when Chancellor of the Exchequer admitted: 'We have been trying to deal with it (the economic situation) by a series of temporary expedients which have led to a series of crises as each expedient became exhausted.' (19th September 1949)

Thus it was that in April 1951 Mr (now Sir) Harold Wilson, when President of the Board of Trade, stated that: 'British industry stands disorganised and threatened by partial paralysis.' (*Hansard*, 24th April 1951)

Inflation

The inevitable consequence of socialist inflationary policies was a rapid and continuous rise in prices. The devaluation of the pound in 1949 increased the rate of inflation which was already too high. Over the whole six years of Labour government prices generally rose by about 40 per cent and food prices alone by over 50 per cent.

This rapid inflation meant that there was no improvement in the buying power of wages. Indeed prices rose faster than wages with, for example, wages rising on average by 11 per cent in the eighteen months between March 1950 and October 1951 as compared with an increase of 14 per cent in prices for the same period.

Taxation

Taxation per head rose on average from £65 10s 6d (£65.52½) in 1944–1945 to £72 17s 6d (£72.87½) in 1950–1951.

Considerable increases were made in all the taxes on goods and services such as purchase tax and the taxes on beer, tobacco etc. In 1951–1952, in the last socialist budget, taxation was estimated to yield roughly £1,000m. more than at the height of the war. By the time the Socialists left office, British taxation was higher than in any country outside the Communist world.

Pensions and benefits

Although the Labour government brought into operation the comprehensive National Insurance Scheme, worked out by the predominantly Conservative wartime coalition administration, inflationary socialist policies robbed this scheme of much of its value. For example, every £1 paid out in pensions and benefits in 1946 had a buying power of only about 15s 0d (75p) by 1951. As Mr Richard Crossman, one time Labour's Secretary of State for the Social Services, admitted, under the Labour government: 'the standard of living of our old people went down. They were cheated even of the modest slice of the national cake which they had been promised.' (*Sunday Pictorial* 7th November 1954)

Health and education

One of the major schemes worked out by the wartime Coalition Government was for a comprehensive National Health Service and the post-war Labour government passed legislation as a result of which the service started together with the National Insurance Scheme in July 1948.

Although on 6th October 1949 Mr Aneurin Bevan categorically stated that the Government had 'set its face against' the whole idea of charges for use of the Service, the National Health Service Amendment Act 1949 provided for a charge for prescriptions from family doctors and in 1951 Labour introduced charges for dentures, and spectacles as part and parcel of economy measures to deal with the economic situation.

Education suffered a series of cuts including one of $12\frac{1}{2}$ per cent in school building in 1949 and charges were raised for school meals and evening classes.

Housing

After promising a house building rate of between 400,000 and 600,000 houses a year, Labour succeeded in only one year – (in 1948 when about 227,000 were built) – in achieving a rate in excess of 200,000. In both the financial crises of 1947 and 1949 housing was one of the chief targets for cuts.

Rationing

When Labour left office meat, bacon, tea, cheese, butter, margarine, cooking fats, eggs, sugar, sweets, and gammon were all strictly rationed and none of these essential goods could be obtained without the surrender of coupons or at any shop (except sweets) other than where the customer was registered. Indeed in January 1949, after nearly four years of socialism the British public were getting in their rations 17 per cent less meat, 75 per cent less bacon and 50 per cent less cheese than they were getting in January 1945 when the war in Europe was in its most intensive stage.

Nationalisation

Labour went ahead with costly nationalisation schemes including coal, gas, electricity, the railways and steel, but these schemes caused more problems than they solved. Typical of the specious socialist promises about the results of nationalisation was the statement by Mr Herbert (later Lord) Morrison who in referring to the electricity industry said that: 'In too many cases electricity is beyond the pocket of the housewife yet it is one of the greatest boons she can have. It can lighten her labours and brighten her day. Only by nationalisation can we make sure that she gets this help cheaply and as a right.'

Thirteen years of record progress

During the thirteen years of Conservative government from 1951–1964, the standard of living of the British people rose by 50 per cent which was more than in the whole of the previous half century. Here are some of the main highlights of progress:

Prices and choice

Prices became much more stable. They rose little more than half as fast as under the post-war Labour government. Between 1958–1964 Britain had one of the best steady-price records in Europe.

Shoppers had greater variety and choice following the ending of rationing by the mid-50s.

Earnings and pensions

Sound economic policies brought a rapid increase in Britain's real wealth – not just paper increases cancelled out by inflation. Earnings and national insurance pensions rose more than twice as fast as prices.

Savings

Savings were encouraged – personal savings totalled nearly £2,000m. in 1964 compared with less than £200m. in 1951 – a more than tenfold increase.

Taxation

Income tax was reduced five times for all taxpayers bringing the standard rate down from 9s 6d (47½p) to 7s 9d (about 39p). The starting point for surtax on earned incomes was raised from £2,000 to £5,000. Millions of people benefited from special tax reliefs for the elderly, widows, the blind, those with dependent relatives, and those responsible for children.

Housing

Conservatives implemented their pledge that 300,000 houses a year would be built – although Labour claimed it would be impossible to build more than 200,000 a year. Thus almost four million new houses were built so that by 1964 one in every four families were living in a new home built under the Conservatives.

The proportion of families owning their own homes increased from about 30 per cent in 1951 to nearly 47 per cent in 1964, and this, together with the increase in personal savings represented real progress towards the property-owning democracy favoured by Conservatives.

Education and health

Some 7,000 new schools were built and over 3,250,000 new places provided. Despite a rise of 1,500,000 in the number of children at school, the number of over-size classes was reduced.

The increase of teachers more than matched the increase in pupils. The number of passes at both GCE 'O' and 'A' levels increased two and a half times.

There was all-round expansion of the health service. The number of family doctors increased by nearly 20 per cent, hospital doctors by 30 per cent and the number of full-time nurses by more than 25 per cent. There was considerable expansion of the local community services so that by 1964 every week on average there was being opened one new training centre and one new hostel for the mentally ill or handicapped, two new maternity and child welfare clinics and two or three community homes for old people. A record hospital building programme was also started.

The strength of the economy

When the Conservatives left office in 1964 the British economy was stronger than ever before in history. Our national income was more than double what it was in 1951 – 40 per cent more in real terms.

Capital investment – the modernisation of British industry – was also running at double the 1951 rate.

The rate of economic growth accelerated: in the six years 1958–1964, the economy grew by 25 per cent.

As a result of earning more abroad than we spent, by 1964 Britain was again a creditor nation and overseas assets were being added to at a rate of £400m. a year. Britain's foreign debts were reduced by nearly £500m. through payments on the £2,250m. borrowed by the 1945–1951 Labour government.

This striking increase in the strength of our economy made possible the record progress in the improvement both of the standard of living of ordinary families and of social services like education, health and the care of the elderly.

1952

The proposals in the newly elected Conservative government's first budget, introduced by **Mr R. A. (now Lord) Butler**, were embodied in the **Finance Act** of this year. The main aims of this budget were to provide incentives to effort and work, to make increased social provision for those in need and to make effective economies in public spending. Thus, some two million people were relieved of income tax altogether while a further fourteen million paid less income tax.

Food subsidies were reduced but at the same time the social

security benefits were improved and of course tax paying families benefited from the income tax reductions.

The increases in pensions, other national insurance benefits, and family allowances announced at the time of the Budget were given effect to by the **Family Allowances and National Insurance Act**. Similar increases in war disability pensions were made by Royal Warrant. The buying power of pensions and national insurance benefits was restored to what it was in July 1948 when the National Insurance Scheme began, thereby repairing much of the damage done by socialist inflationary policies. The family allowance was increased from 5s (25p) a week to 8s (40p) a week.

The **Pensions (Increase) Act** benefited some 320,000 public service pensioners such as retired civil servants, teachers and other local government employees by improving their pensions.

The **Export Guarantees Act** helped our export trade by improving the guarantees provided by the Board of Trade in connection with the export, manufacture or other matters which encouraged exports.

The **National Health Service Act** brought in charges for dental treatment with provision for exemption in the case of children, expectant and nursing mothers. It also brought in charges for medicines and appliances provided at hospital outpatients' departments with exemptions in the case of war pensioners being treated for their disabilities and those on national assistance. These charges were necessary in order to keep down health service spending to what could be afforded without impeding progress in making better provision for urgent needs.

The **Pneumoconiosis and Byssinosis Benefit Act** provided for the payment of benefit out of the Industrial Injuries Fund to certain persons who were totally disabled or had died (in which case benefit became payable to their dependants) from pneumoconiosis or byssinosis after 31st December 1949 and who were not eligible for benefit under any of the existing arrangements.

The **Licensed Premises in New Towns Act** repealed that part of Labour's 1949 Licensing Act which provided for the state management of the liquor trade in new towns.

Private members measures introduced by Conservatives included the **Heating Appliances (Fireguards) Act** which ensured electric and gas fires and oil stoves were not sold unless they were fitted with adequate guards; the **Corneal Grafting Act** which made it possible for eyes for corneal grafting to be bequeathed; and the **Affiliation Orders Act** which brought the law relating to the maintenance of children born out of wedlock into line with that for legitimate children (when the father has deserted the mother and child) in regard to the maximum amount that may be ordered for maintenance by a magistrates court and the age up to which maintenance may be payable.

1953

The **Transport Act,** 1953, provided for the denationalisation of road haulage and embodied proposals for the decentralisation of railway administration. The aim of the Act was to increase the flexibility and efficiency of goods transport as a whole, and to allow road and rail to compete more freely on the basis of quality of service. The denationalisation of iron and steel was provided for by the **Iron and Steel Act** of this year.

Mr Butler's second budget proposals were implemented by this year's **Finance Act** and the principal aim was to continue the process of reducing the burden of taxation, giving greater reward to effort and greater incentive to industry. The standard rate of income tax was reduced from 9s 6d (47½p) to 9s (45p) and reductions were also made in the lower rates of tax*; all round reductions of about 25 per cent were made in purchase tax; improvements were made in the depreciation allowances available to industry and provision was made for the abolition of the excess profits tax.

The **Monopolies and Restrictive Practices Commission Act** strengthened the Monopolies Commission in order to enable it to deal with a greater number of references at any one time.

The **National Insurance Act** of this year improved the system of maternity benefits provided under the National Insurance Scheme. In particular it ensured that a woman who decided to have her baby at home would not be materially worse off than a woman going into hospital for her confinement.

The **National Insurance (Industrial Injuries) Act** made a number of improvements in the industrial injuries scheme. In particular it enabled about 8,000 more people a year – about one-tenth of the number of claimants – to qualify for benefit.

The **Education (Miscellaneous Provisions) Act** made a number of changes in the arrangements for Exchequer assistance to the voluntary schools, the majority of which are run by religious denominations. These changes were therefore of particular benefit to the Churches.

The **School Crossing Patrols Act** improved the safety of school children by making special provision for the control of traffic by persons other than police constables at places where children cross roads on their way to and from school.

The **Prevention of Crime Act** made it a punishable offence for a person to be found with a cosh or a similar offensive weapon in a public place without very good reason.

* No valid comparison with a person's tax liability in 1976 can be made by comparing basic income tax rates. In 1976 people paid more income tax than ever before because under the Labour government the personal tax allowances lagged far behind the rate of inflation.

1954

The **Finance Act** of this year embodied the proposals in Mr Butler's third budget. This budget contained no tax increases and no new taxes. It continued the process of helping industry by improving investment allowances in order to assist modernisation. Death duties on both family businesses and small estates were reduced. Post-war credits became payable to heirs at the time when the original holder would have reached the qualifying age. Purchase tax was reduced on a wide range of goods such as electric fires and washing machines.

The **Atomic Energy Authority Act** established the Atomic Energy Authority to be responsible for atomic energy. The Authority took over from the Government the factories and laboratories working on atomic energy and producing fissile materials.

The **Electricity Reorganisation (Scotland) Act** reorganised the administration of the electricity industry in Scotland by, amongst other measures, transferring the powers of the Ministry of Fuel and Power in relation to electricity to the Secretary of State for Scotland.

The **Mines and Quarries Act** of this year brought up to date the safety and health provisions in the mines in the light of the recommendation of the pre-war Royal Commission appointed in 1935 and the growth of technical knowledge which has since taken place. This was the tenth principal measure governing health and safety conditions in mines since the famous Act of 1842 inspired by Lord Shaftesbury (see page 11). This 1954 Act replaced the Act of 1911 introduced by Sir Winston Churchill, then Home Secretary in Mr Asquith's Liberal government – a measure which had proved very successful in reducing the number of accidents in the mining industry.

The **Baking Industry (Hours of Work) Act** restricted the amount of night work in the baking industry.

The **Cotton Act** provided for the winding up of the Raw Cotton Commission thereby enabling the Liverpool Cotton Exchange to re-open in May of this year. The Raw Cotton Commission had been established as the monopoly purchaser by the Labour government in 1947.

The **National Insurance Act** of this year more than restored the damage done by socialist inflation. It raised pensions and national insurance benefits to a level which gave them a buying power in excess of the value intended in 1946 when, under the National Insurance Acts of that year, the rates were fixed in broad accordance with the proposals of the wartime Coalition Government. Similar improvements were made in war disability pensions by Royal Warrant. The new weekly rates of benefit under the 1954 Act were 50 per cent above the 1946 rates whereas prices had risen by 44 per cent since 1946.

The **Industrial Diseases (Benefit) Act** provided for the payment of benefit at the cost of the Industrial Injuries Insurance Fund to certain persons partially disabled from pneumoconiosis or byssinosis who were not covered by the Workmen's Compensation Acts or the National Insurance (Industrial Injuries) Acts.

The **Teachers (Superannuation) Act** made a number of improvements in the benefits provided under the teachers superannuation scheme and adjusted contributions in order to put the scheme on a sound financial footing.

The **Royal Irish Constabulary (Widows' Pensions) Act** provided for the payment of supplementary allowances and of pensions to persons who were, or had been, widows of certain former members of the Royal Irish Constabulary.

The **Food and Drugs Amendment Act** provided for the greater protection of the public against the sale of foods containing injurious ingredients and against the misleading descriptions of food and drugs in labels and advertisements.

The **Housing (Repairs and Rents) Act** improved the conditions under which owners of houses could qualify for grants to modernise or improve their property. This measure brought about a major increase in the pace of house improvement with no less than nearly 8,000 houses being improved in the first four months after the passing of the Act as compared with an average of only about 2,000 a year over the previous five years. This measure together with its Scottish counterpart, **The Housing (Repairs and Rents) (Scotland) Act,** started what was known as 'Operation Rescue' to deal with the many older houses which were capable of being improved and modernised. This operation started at a time when the building of new houses was going ahead at the rate of over 300,000 a year so fully implementing the Conservative pledge made during the 1951 General Election.

The **Landlord and Tenant Act** of this year extended the protection of the Rent Acts to residential leaseholders of ground leases of more than twenty-one years when their leases expired. The Act provided that landlords could regain their houses only if their need was proved to be greater than the tenants' need or if they intended to redevelop their property. The landlord had to come to an agreement with the tenant about a fair market rent and the repair of the property. In addition the Act gave business and professional tenants the right to apply to the courts for a renewed tenancy at a fair market rent when their leases expired.

The **Long Leases (Scotland) Act** gave all lessees under pre-1914 ground leases the right, during a period of five years to claim 'feu title'.

The **Television Act** provided for the start of independent television with the setting up of the Independent Television Authority.

A Conservative Private Members Act – **Rights of Entry (Gas and**

Electricity Boards) Act – provided, that except in cases of emergency, entry into private premises, without the consent of the occupier, by inspectors of gas and electricity boards, should only be exercised if a warrant has been obtained from a justice of the peace.

1955

There were two **Finance Acts** in 1955; the first embodying the proposals contained in Mr Butler's April budget and the second, implementing the provisions of Mr Butler's October budget.

The April budget imposed no new taxes and no tax increases. It reduced the standard rate of income tax by 6d (2½p) in the £ from 9s (45p) to 8s 6d (42½p) with corresponding reductions in the lower tax rates. And there were also increases in the various personal tax allowances. These income tax reductions benefited all the seventeen million income tax payers and relieved two and a half million of them completely from income tax.

The purposes of the October budget were to continue the process of bringing about economies in public spending and to restrain consumption. Thus, the rates of purchase tax were increased. By 1955 government expenditure accounted for 26 per cent of the national income as compared with 29 per cent in 1951, when Labour left office. The October budget envisaged the phasing out of the Exchequer subsidy for new council houses except in the case of slum clearance and the relief of congested towns, and the legislation to give effect to this change was introduced in November of this year.

The **Children and Young Persons (Harmful Publications) Act** dealt with the problem of what had become known as 'horror comics' which were defined as 'any book, magazine or other like work which consisted wholly or mainly of stories told in pictures (with or without the addition of written matter), being stories portraying:

(*a*) the commission of crimes; or

(*b*) acts of violence or cruelty; or

(*c*) incidents of a repulsive or horrible nature:

in such a way that the work as a whole would tend to corrupt a child or young person into whose hands it might fall (whether by inciting or encouraging him to commit crimes or acts of violence or cruelty or in any other way whatsoever).'

The **Requisitioned Houses and Housing (Amendment) Act** provided for the ending of the wartime requisitioning powers for housing purposes over a period of five years and secured the early release of requisitioned houses whose owners had urgent need of them.

The **Food and Drugs Act** provided an up-to-date code for food in the light of modern knowledge.

1956

The proposals contained in Mr Harold Macmillan's first budget were embodied in the **Finance Act** of this year. The main aim of this budget was to enable Britain to pay her way in the world by building up her industrial strength which meant restraining consumption at home. The budget therefore concentrated on encouraging savings. New issues of National Savings Certificates were provided for and the Premium Bond was started. Special tax relief became available for the self-employed and others not covered by group pension schemes. They obtained the same tax relief on their contributions towards pension provision as those covered by a group scheme. Reductions were made in the stamp duty on house purchase. Provision was made for the ending of the bread subsidy, but this was to be timed to coincide with increases in the family allowances for third and subsequent children.

The **Coal Industry Act** increased the limit of the Coal Board's borrowing powers to enable the Board to reorganise and develop the industry with the aim of boosting production.

The **Restrictive Trade Practices Act** was generally recognised as the most far reaching attack on restrictive practices connected with the supply of goods ever made in this country. It provided for the establishment of a special Restrictive Practices Division of the High Court to determine whether or not the practices registered were in the public interest. It also provided for the formation of a smaller and more compact Monopolies Commission. The Conservative Party has always believed that free and fair competition is infinitely preferable to nationalisation and rigid State control. This Act was concerned to ensure observance of the discipline of genuine competition.

The **Agriculture (Safety, Health and Welfare Provisions) Act** provided for farm workers what earlier Conservative legislation had done for the other main branches of productive industry – by the Factories Act of 1937 and the Mines and Quarries Act of 1954. It provided for a comprehensive code of safety regulations to protect farm workers in the light of the recommendations of the Gowers Committee on Health, Welfare and Safety in Non-industrial Employments.

The **Family Allowances and National Insurance Act** of this year provided for improvements in the allowances for children paid with widows benefits under the National Insurance scheme. In this way it was recognised that widows with children to support needed special help. This Act also increased the weekly rate of family allowances from 8s (40p) to 10s (50p) for third and subsequent children in accordance with the Chancellor of the Exchequer's announcement in his budget speech. It was also provided that family allowances could be paid in respect of children up to the age of eighteen if they were still at school, or apprenticed, whereas formerly they ceased at the age of sixteen.

The **Workmen's Compensation and Benefit (Supplementation) Act** increased the benefits payable to totally incapacitated persons covered by the old Workmen's Compensation Scheme.

The **Pensions (Increase) Act** and the corresponding Royal Warrant for the service pensions, increased by 10 per cent the pensions of some 400,000 retired public servants and members of the armed forces and their dependants. This Act removed certain income tests which had prevented many pensioners from benefiting from earlier measures.

The **Teachers (Superannuation) Act** improved the pension benefits payable to teachers and provided for the Exchequer to take over the accumulated deficit in the teachers' pension fund; this improvement in teachers' pensions followed the start in 1955 of the introduction of equal pay within the teaching profession.

The **Dentists Act** of this year provided for the setting up of a General Dental Council thereby enabling the profession to become self-governing. Under the Act the powers formerly exercised by the Dental Board and certain powers exercised by the General Medical Council were transferred to the newly created General Dental Council.

It also provided for the training and eventual use of dental ancillary workers to carry out specified work.

The **Housing Subsidies Act** implemented the intention announced in the budget speech to concentrate the Exchequer housing subsidies on new council houses provided for priority groups. Thus, the general needs subsidy was abolished for new council houses and so far as new council housing was concerned subsidies became available only for slum clearance, for the relief of congested towns and for one-bedroomed houses suitable for the elderly.

The **Food and Drugs (Scotland) Act** provided for an up-to-date code relating to clean food similar to that provided for in England and Wales by the Food and Drugs Act 1955.

The **Clean Air Act** contained comprehensive provisions for dealing with the problems of air pollution. This Act was based on the final report of the Beaver Committee set up in July 1953 which estimated that air pollution was costing as much as £250m. a year. This measure enabled local authorities to declare Smoke Control Areas.

The **Road Traffic Act** provided for the compulsory examination of older motor vehicles (steering, brakes, lighting, etc.) and brought pedal cyclists within the law for dangerous or careless driving and driving under the influence of drink.

The **Police, Fire and Probation Officers Remuneration Act** made it possible for pay awards to the police, fire and probation officers to be back-dated.

A Conservative Private Members measure, the **National Insurance Act**, increased the amount which a pensioner could earn without any reduction in his retirement pension from £2 a week to £2 10s (£2.50) and also relaxed the arrangements for deductions in the case of earnings above the limit. The broad effect was that a pensioner could earn £5 10s (£5.50) a week without losing his entire pension as against £4 previously.

1957

The **Finance Act** of this year embodied the proposals of Mr Peter (now Lord) Thorneycroft's first budget. The great success of the October 1956 budget, which encouraged savings, enabled Mr Thorneycroft to resume the process of all-round tax reductions. The tax allowances for the family man were improved and so too were the special tax reliefs for the elderly. Reductions were made in the purchase tax on a variety of household goods. The entertainment tax on the theatre and sport was abolished and it was greatly simplified in its application to cinemas.

The **Electricity Act** provided for the reorganisation of the electricity supply industry in England and Wales and was based on recommendations made by the Herbert Committee, set up in October 1954, to enquire into the operation of the electricity supply industry. In particular the Act created a Central Electricity Generating Board to take over the responsibilities for generating and delivering electricity in bulk; it was expected that this body would devote a large part of its time to the construction of nuclear power stations.

The **Coal Mining (Subsidence) Act** required the National Coal Board to repair physical damage caused by mining subsidence to land, buildings, structures (including roads, railways, aircraft runways, etc.) and works such as sewers, drains and other service lines and pipes which suffered.

The **Agriculture Act** of this year enabled farmers to plan ahead more confidently by removing uncertainty about guaranteed prices. The Act also provided a comprehensive range of grants for improvement to farms and farm buildings. In addition the Act established a Pig Industry Development Authority with wide powers for securing improvements in production, processing and distribution of pig meat.

The **Customs Duties (Dumping and Subsidies) Act** gave the Board of Trade power to impose duties to give protection against imports 'dumped' from foreign countries.

The **National Insurance Act** benefited in various ways about 250,000 people. Its main provisions were:
    (*a*) retirement and widow pensioners under the age of 70 (65 for women) were enabled to revoke their declaration of retirement

if they so wished and thus earn additions to their retirement pensions paid when they ceased to work;

(*b*) the amount which a wife could earn without her husband losing entitlement to dependency benefit for her when he was sick or unemployed was doubled from £1 to £2 a week;

(*c*) a new Special Child Allowance became available for the mother of the children of a dissolved marriage on the death of the ex-husband if he was contributing to her upkeep.

The **National Insurance (No. 2) Act** of this year provided for all round increases in national insurance and industrial injury benefits with similar improvements in war disability pensions provided by Royal Warrant. The effect of these increases was that a single rate pension was in real terms worth 12s 1d (over 60p) more than in 1951 when Labour left office.

The **Rent Act** of this year had as its main purpose the improvement of privately rented housing and it therefore provided for the charging of more realistic rents. It freed from the rent control and security of tenure provisions of earlier Rent Acts all new lettings and existing lettings as they became vacant. It also removed rent control and security of tenure from privately rented houses with a high rateable value. The Act provided for a transitional period during which tenants of houses with high rateable values subject to decontrol would continue to have security of tenure. In addition this Act provided that the rents of houses remaining controlled under the Rent Acts would be increased to more realistic levels. The immediate effect of the Act was that six out of seven privately rented homes remained subject to rent control, but the provision for decontrol as vacant possession occurred gradually increased the proportion to which the controls of the Rent Acts no longer applied.

The **Housing and Town Development (Scotland) Act** provided for a system of Scottish housing subsidies which took greater account of needs. It replaced the previous arrangements under which the subsidy varied according to the size of the house by a system which gave extra help to the provision of new council housing to assist congested cities, particularly Glasgow and new towns. The new system also encouraged the provision of more small council houses of which there was a considerable need to meet the special requirements of the elderly.

The **Advertisements (Hire-Purchase) Act,** a Conservative Private Members measure, safeguarded buyers against misleading advertisements and ensured that full details of deposits and instalments are given in respect of any transaction.

1958

The **Finance Act** of this year embodied the proposals contained in Mr Derick Heathcoat Amory's first budget. This budget made all-round reductions in purchase tax and improved the special tax reliefs for the elderly. It also encouraged industrial expansion by improving the initial tax allowances for plant and machinery.

The **Distribution of Industry (Industrial Finance) Act** of this year adapted the system started under the 1945 Act to meet the needs of areas with an unemployment rate above the average.

The **Agriculture Act** amended the 1947 Act by repealing the disciplinary powers to supervise and dispossess farmers and created conditions in which the landlord-tenant system could work more effectively.

The **Local Government Act** aimed to give greater independence to local authorities in England and Wales through stronger financial resources, more convenient areas and increased responsibilities for the lower-tier councils in districts and boroughs. This Act improved the system of local government finance by providing for a new general grant (sometimes called a block grant) to replace a number of percentage or specific grants which had been tied to particular services, and the most important of these services covered by this new general grant were education (other than school milk and meals), health and welfare, fire services and child care. The main advantages of the new general grant were first, that it gave local authorities more freedom to spend their monies according to the needs of their areas and second, that it cut out a great deal of the checking procedures previously required under the percentage grants and so simplified administration. The Act also provided for the setting up of two Commissions (for England and Wales respectively) with the function of revising the areas of local government.

The **Local Government and Miscellaneous Financial Provisions (Scotland) Act** provided for a general grant for Scottish local authorities similar to that provided for English and Welsh local authorities by the Local Government Act. The Scottish Act did not however provide for a review of local government areas in Scotland as there was no general demand for this.

The **Water Act** gave water undertakings in Great Britain statutory powers to take supplies from lakes, rivers and other sources not normally used, in cases of extreme shortage due to drought.

The **Children Act** of this year laid a more positive duty on local authorities to ensure the well-being of foster children and put more emphasis on protection by enabling a local authority to prevent a child being received into an unsuitable foster home. The Act also improved the law of adoption in the light of recommendations made by the Hurst Committee which had reported in September 1954. It was made clear that local authorities could arrange adoptions of any children, whether in their care or not.

The **Maintenance Orders Act** enabled maintenance orders to be enforced by requiring, in the event of non-payment, the husband's employer to make a deduction from the man's salary or wage.

The **Physical Training and Recreation Act** enabled local authorities to make loans for physical training and recreation.

The **Tribunals and Inquiries Act** enacted many of the recommendations of the Franks Committee. In particular it provided for an Advisory Council to keep the constitution and working of administrative tribunals constantly under review and for appeals to the courts against the decisions of tribunals.

There were two Conservative Private Members measures; first, the **Litter Act** which made the spreading of litter an offence punishable by fine. And second, there was the **Opticians Act** which provided a recognised status for opticians by registration to protect the public against unqualified and untrained persons posing as opticians.

1959

The **Finance Act** of this year embodied the proposals in Mr Heathcoat Amory's second budget. Mr Heathcoat Amory defined the main purpose of this budget as being to 'invigorate and improve the strength and competitiveness of our national economy'. The standard rate of income tax was reduced from 8s 6d (42½p) to 7s 9d (about 39p) with corresponding cuts in the reduced rates. There were all round reductions in purchase tax, and the tax allowances for industry were improved.

The **Income Tax (Repayment of Post-War Credits) Act** implemented the proposals announced in the budget speech for speeding up the repayment of post-war credits by

(*a*) lowering the qualifying age for repayment from 65 to 63 for men and from 60 to 58 for women;

(*b*) by providing for immediate payment in certain clearly defined cases of hardship and

(*c*) by providing for immediate payment to heirs of deceased holders irrespective of age or circumstances. In addition the Act provided for interest to be paid in respect of outstanding credits.

The **Nuclear Installations (Licensing and Insurance) Act** controlled, in the interests of safety, the building and operation of nuclear reactors by licensing, and imposed upon any one granted such a licence absolute liability for all damage incurred.

The **Cotton Industry Act** of this year provided for Exchequer help for the reorganisation of the cotton industry on a viable financial basis with special grants for modernisation.

The **Agriculture (Small Farmers) Act** provided for special schemes of assistance to small farmers with the aim of bringing about a lasting improvement in the economic position of these farms. By 1964 nearly 50,000 applications for grants under this Act had been approved.

The **National Insurance Act** of this year provided for contributions graduated according to earnings to be paid on top of the flat rate contribution by employed people except the lower paid. These graduated contributions gave entitlement to additions over and above the basic pension. Those covered by occupational pension schemes could be contracted out of this new graduated state scheme which started in April 1961. The effect of this Act was to put state pensions on a sounder financial basis by ensuring that the income of the National Insurance Scheme increased as earnings rose. It also enabled the Exchequer subsidy to the scheme to be largely concentrated on the lower paid whose proportionate share of the cost of benefits was reduced. The Act also gave a considerable boost to the expansion of occupational pension schemes. The Labour Party strongly opposed this Act and tried to pretend that the new scheme was a swindle. But, Mr Douglas (now Lord) Houghton, formerly Labour Member of Parliament for Sowerby and one time Chairman of the Labour Party as well as an acknowledged expert on pension matters, gave the lie to this nonsense when he said: 'I hope that we will stop talking about "the Tory swindle"; it does not happen to be true.' (*Hansard*, 4th December 1969)

The **National Assistance Act** raised the amounts of savings and income which a person could have and still be eligible for national assistance.

The **Pensions (Increase) Act** provided for increases in the pensions of some 415,000 former public servants (or their widows or dependants).

The purpose of the **Mental Health Act** was that mental illness should be regarded in the same spirit as physical illness, and that people suffering from mental illness should be encouraged to seek treatment promptly, voluntarily and with no more formality than in the case of physical illness. While retaining such compulsory powers of admission and detention as were considered to be necessary in the interests of both the public and the patient, and while providing new appeal procedures in such cases, the Act removed a number of restrictions on informal admission. As a result nearly all admissions to mental hospitals became voluntary and informal.

The **House Purchase and Housing Act** was specifically designed to help those who wanted to buy their own homes, but found the deposit a major stumbling block. The Act helped in two ways; first, by enabling local councils to advance up to 100 per cent of valuation as against the former limit of 90 per cent; and second, by enabling those wanting to buy older houses within certain price limits to obtain advances of up to 95 per cent of the purchase price from building societies under arrangements agreed between the Government and those societies participating in the scheme. The Act also enabled all house owners to qualify as of right for what became known as 'standard grants' for certain basic amenities (a bath, a wash-hand basin, a hot water supply, a water closet, and a food store). In addition the Act improved the qualifying conditions for the then existing improvement grants available at the discretion of local councils for the improvement and modernisation of older houses. This Act greatly increased the number of older houses improved with the aid of grants. In 1962 alone, for example, 115,000 houses were improved with the help of grants (including over 70,000 standard grants) as compared with just over 38,000 in 1957. The scheme enabling people buying older houses to get 95 per cent of the purchase price under certain conditions from building societies continued until July 1961 by which time not far short of £100m. had been advanced for this purpose.

The **New Towns Act** of this year as well as increasing the money available for new towns, set up a New Towns Commission to take over some of the assets of the existing new towns in order to avoid placing monopoly ownership in the hands of local councils.

The **Town and Country Planning Act** was a major step in removing injustice and clearing up the mess resulting from the financial provisions of the socialist 1947 Planning Act. Its main effect was to provide for market value compensations to be paid where land was compulsorily acquired.

The **Education Act** improved the Exchequer grants available to the voluntary schools, most of which were run by religious denominations.

The **Street Offences Act** of this year was remarkably successful in greatly reducing the problem of soliciting for immoral purposes in the streets. It substantially increased fines for this offence with imprisonment as a possible penalty for repeated offences.

The **Landlord and Tenant (Furniture and Fittings) Act,** a Conservative Private Members' measure, made it an offence to ask for a concealed premium on furniture and fittings before any transactions between landlord and tenant have taken place. It also gave local councils power to inspect furniture and fittings after serving due notice on the person offering them for sale.

1960

The proposals in Mr Heathcoat-Amory's third budget were embodied in the **Finance Act** of this year. In his budget speech Mr Heathcoat-Amory pointed out that 'the standard of living of the nation had never been so high' and that the need now was to 'consolidate and fortify this prosperity'. The budget therefore was a cautious one. The various tax reliefs for those with special needs were improved and a new tax allowance was introduced for people responsible for children who had lost one or both parents. The hardship grounds whereby immediate repayment of post-war credits could be obtained were widened enabling more to qualify. Entertainments Duty was completely abolished.

The **Local Employment Act** of this year implemented the pledge in the 1959 Conservative General Election Manifesto that there would be early legislation to strengthen the Government's powers for dealing with unemployment. Under this Act new and more effective powers were taken to concentrate help on areas where unemployment was above the average. The new rules were made more flexible so that districts meriting assistance could be added to the list as occasion required. In these districts of high unemployment, known as development areas, the Board of Trade could either build factories for sale or lease to industrialists or they could assist firms to build their own factories by way of loan or grant. In addition assistance was provided for financial help to be given to workers moving to areas where jobs were available.

The **Dock Workers (Pension) Act** facilitated the introduction of a pension scheme for dock workers.

The **Payment of Wages Act** of this year made it possible for wages to be paid by means of a postal or money order or direct to a bank account where wage earners preferred this to receiving wages in cash.

The **Horticulture Act** provided for the introduction of new grants to horticulture and the establishment of the Horticultural Marketing Council. The grants were to help the industry to improve the grading, packing and presentation of market products and generally to aid and advance the growers' side of the market business.

The **Civil Aviation (Licensing Act)** ensured proper standards of safety by requiring all who provided public transport by air to hold an air operator's certificate. Previously this was not obligatory for operators of air charter services. The Act also set up an independent Licensing Board charged with issuing licences to run air transport services for which all airline operators could apply on an equal footing. The monopoly granted to the Air Corporations under the Air Corporations Act 1949 had long ceased to exist in practice and was finally abolished under this Act.

The **National Insurance Act** of this year provided for all-round increases in benefits under the National Insurance and Industrial Injuries Schemes with similar improvements in war disability pensions made by Royal Warrant. These improvements gave a further increase in the buying power of benefits. For, while the increase in benefits amounted to about 15 per cent since the previous increase in 1958, the rise in prices since 1958 had been only 7 per cent and the rise in average wages had been about 12 per cent. In addition the Act abolished the rule whereby, quite apart from earnings, a person could not be regarded as retired and therefore entitled to the retirement pension if he worked for more than twelve hours a week.

The **Mental Health (Scotland) Act** of this year made similar provisions in Scotland to that provided in England and Wales by the Mental Health Act 1959.

The **Professions Supplementary to Medicine Act** gave professional status to chiropodists, dieticians, medical and laboratory technicians, occupational therapists, radiographers and remedial gymnasts. The Act provided for the registration of present practitioners and of future entrants; and for approved qualifications and courses of training.

The **Charities Act** of this year, which was the first major legislation in this field for almost a century, implemented the majority of the recommendations of the Nathan Committee Report of 1952. Social progress had in many cases overtaken the traditional objects of charity. This measure was designed to modernise the administration of charity on the basis of partnership within the framework of the Welfare State, while still maintaining its freedom from political pressure.

The **Legal Aid Act** of this year was the first major revision of the Legal Aid Scheme since it started in 1949. It increased the amounts of both income and capital which a person could have and still qualify for legal aid.

The **Road Traffic and Roads Improvement Act** provided for the introduction of ticket fines as a voluntary alternative to court procedure for parking offences. It also made provision for traffic wardens to help the police in road traffic control.

The **Radioactive Substances Act** made provision for controlling the storage of radioactive materials and the safe disposal of waste products. The increasing use of radioactive substances made it necessary for all premises, as well as those of the Atomic Energy Authority and other nuclear power installations, to be controlled on a national basis.

The **Caravan Sites and Control of Development Act** stemmed from the recommendations of the Arton Wilson Report of 1959. This Act ensured that before land could be used for the purpose of a caravan site, a licence must be obtained from the local council. The aim was to ensure that reasonable standards of safety, sanitation and amenity were provided on caravan sites.

The **Betting and Gaming Act** followed closely the recommendations of the Royal Commission on Betting, Lotteries and Gaming published in March 1951, and its broad aim was to allow reasonable freedom for people who wished to bet or play games for money while at the same time retaining sufficient safeguards to act as deterrents against excess. As regards betting, the Act provided for betting shops to be established under licences granted by local Justices. The Act permitted factory runners, but street betting remained illegal, and the provision of reasonable opportunities for legal betting enabled the police to deal with it much more effectively. For gaming, the Act provided simple rules. Nobody under 18 could take part, the game had to be fair as between players, there was to be no 'cut' on the stakes for the benefit of the organisers and (except for clubs) there was to be no charge for the right to take part. The use of gaming machines, known as 'fruit machines' was restricted to clubs.

A number of Conservative Private Members measures reached the statute book during this year. The **Public Bodies (Admission to Meetings) Act** which was sponsored by Mrs Margaret Thatcher, who had been elected as Conservative member for Finchley at the 1959 General Election, gave the Press a general right of admission to meetings of public bodies except where there were special reasons of confidentiality why they should not be present. The need for this measure had been made clear by the exclusion of the Press from the meetings of certain councils during the 1958 Printing Strike. Other Conservative Private Members measures included:

(1) The **Noise Abatement Act** provided that unreasonable noise would become a statutory nuisance under the Public Health Acts.

(2) The **Oil Burners (Standard) Act** provided for safety standards for oil heaters and burners.

(3) The **Marriage (Enabling) Act** enabled a person to marry certain kin of a former spouse; for example a man could marry the sister of his former wife.

(4) The **Abandonment of Animals Act** prohibited the abandonment of animals. Previously this was an offence only where actual suffering was caused.

1961

Mr Selwyn Lloyd's first budget proposals were contained in the **Finance Act** of this year. In his budget speech Mr Selwyn Lloyd made the point that more was being earned, more was being spent and more was being saved than ever before. There had however been a deficit in the balance of payments in 1960/61 and the purpose of this budget was summed up by Mr Selwyn Lloyd as follows:

> 'The purposes of the budget have been to maintain investment, to make room for exports, to give a dynamic new incentive to those people who have high responsibility and upon whom so much depends, at the same time, indicating very clearly to those overseas who watch our fortunes that we mean to ensure the stability of the £ sterling at home and abroad.' (Broadcast, 17th April 1961)

Motor vehicle licences were increased and so was the duty on heavy oils; a new duty at 10 per cent was levied on television advertisements. The rate of excess profits tax was increased, but the earnings limit for surtax liability was raised from £2,000 to £5,000 in order to provide more incentive at higher management levels. In addition the Finance Act gave the Government power to increase or reduce all the main revenue duties by up to 10 per cent without the need for legislation.

The **Trustees Investments Act** removed the legal compulsion on trustees to invest trust funds in fixed interest securities (mainly government stock). Under this Act they were enabled to invest up to half the property in a wider range of securities (mainly good equity shares).

The **Covent Garden Market Act** had as its object the prevention of the spread of market activities in the Covent Garden district and the creation of a modern market with up-to-date mechanical handling and storage facilities. The Act created a Market Authority to acquire the market properties owned by Covent Garden Market Limited, provide better facilities, and concentrate activities in a more compact area.

The **Family Allowances and National Insurance Act** made certain improvements in both the national insurance and the industrial injuries schemes and also in the family allowances system. As regards national insurance, improvements were made in the retirement pension increments which could be earned by certain widows; married women separated from their husbands could now get the full standard rates of sickness and unemployment benefit; and certain improvements were made in the child special allowance. The scope of the industrial injuries insurance scheme was extended to cover certain additional risks; the qualifying conditions for the unemployability supplement were eased; and further help was provided for some 20,000 people covered by workmen's compensation. Under this Act children incapable of regular employment because of long-term disability were enabled to qualify for family allowances and for child dependancy benefits under the national insurance scheme up to the age of 16 whether or not they were able to attend school.

The **Public Health Act** gave local authorities a number of well-precedented powers in the field of public health and safety; it replaced the system of prescribing and relaxing building bye-laws by a system of building regulations. In the words of Sir Keith Joseph, one of the Ministers then responsible for Health, the miscellaneous subjects included in this Act range from 'rags to rinks, from cellars to chimneys, from skiing to skittles, and from pigeons to parks'.

The **Human Tissue Act** authorised, subject to a number of reasonable safeguards, the removal of parts of human bodies after death for use for therapeutic purposes and purposes of medical education or research. It also clarified the law regarding post mortem examinations and permitted the cremation of bodies removed for anatomical examination.

The **Suicide Act** provided that it was no longer a crime for a person to attempt suicide. But it remained an offence for a person to aid, abet, counsel or procure the suicide or attempted suicide of another person.

The **Housing Act** of this year reorganised the system of housing subsidies in England and Wales to take account of the fact that after ten years of intensive house building under successive Conservative governments the housing needs of different areas varied considerably – in some areas housing needs were nearly satisfied whereas other areas still had a big housing problem to deal with. Accordingly a subsidy was provided for all new council houses built for approved need, but the amount of subsidy depended upon the financial resources of the local authorities concerned. Those local authorities whose financial resources were deemed to be insufficient received the higher subsidy of £24 a year per house whereas other local authorities received the lower subsidy of £8 a year per house. In addition local authorities were given new and improved powers to deal with houses in multi-occupation.

The **Rating and Valuation Act** provided for the full rating of industry and freight transport and gave charities a 50 per cent mandatory relief from rates with local authorities having the power to remit the balance.

The **Licensing Act** of this year provided for more flexible licensing hours to suit the needs of different areas in England and Wales. The Act also improved the arrangements for the registration of clubs in order to deal with the 'bogus' clubs. At the same time the Act strengthened the provisions for the protection of young people, by, for example, increasing the penalty for knowingly selling drink to any person under 18. It also made it a direct offence to consume alcohol on licensed premises if under 18 as well as being supplied with alcohol at off-licences. Finally, the Act ended a number of irritating anomalies; for example, it ended the ban on the playing of billiards on Sundays in public houses.

The **Criminal Justice Act** improved the penal training for young offenders, with the ultimate aim of ensuring that all persons under

21 were given rigorous training in borstals, detention centres, etc, instead of mixing with hardened criminals in prison. Under this Act provision was made for borstal to be followed by a period of compulsory supervision and this was also applied to detention centres. A number of penalties, particularly those for offences committed by children and young persons were substantially increased.

The **Betting Levy Act** provided for a levy to be paid by bookmakers carrying on a business in connection with horse racing; the proceeds of this levy were devoted to improvements in racehorse breeding, prize money and race-course amenities.

The **Trusts (Scotland) Act** enabled the courts in Scotland to vary the purposes of a trust on behalf of those who were under age, unborn or who for some other reason could not approve for themselves.

The **Flood Prevention (Scotland) Act** gave Scottish local authorities specific powers, which formerly they did not have, to carry out flood prevention work in urban areas under schemes approved by the Secretary of State.

The **Local Authorities (Expenditure on Special Purposes) (Scotland) Act** enabled local authorities in Scotland to make grants to charities, certain non-profit making organisations and funds raised for special purposes, such as the victims of a disaster happening anywhere in Scotland. This Act was passed because it was brought to light that under the previous law local authorities could contribute only where there would result some direct and tangible benefit to their districts.

Conservative Private Members measures included:
(1) The **Home Safety Act** which extended to small local authorities the powers already enjoyed by county and county borough councils to undertake home safety education and to contribute to home safety.
(2) The **Companies (Floating Charges) (Scotland) Act** which enabled firms in Scotland to raise loan capital on the security of their moveable assets – for example their stock in trade such as moveable machinery and so on.

1962

The proposals contained in Mr Selwyn Lloyd's second budget were embodied in the 1962 **Finance Act.** This budget had three main aims:
(1) To set the stage for expansion of exports and thus for sound economic growth;
(2) To modernise our tax system and make it more fair;
(3) To give some help to the elderly and those living on small fixed incomes.

Mr Selwyn Lloyd said that he had set in hand an examination to see whether the system of company taxation could be simplified by having a single corporation tax in place of income and profits tax. The special tax reliefs for the elderly and others on small incomes were improved. Short-term speculative gains were made subject to income and surtax if they were made by individuals, and profits tax if they were made by companies. The rates of estate duty were reduced and the exemption limit for small estates was increased. Most rates of purchase tax were reduced and the system was simplified in order to iron-out anomalies.

In the course of his budget speech Mr Selwyn Lloyd referred to the setting up of the National Economic Development Council (NEDC) and went on to say: 'It is a great experiment. Employers, trade unionists, Cabinet Ministers, independents, men of differing political approaches, differing responsibilities, trying to work together to improve our economic performance.'

The **International Monetary Fund Act** of this year authorised Britain to join with nine other countries in a scheme to make extra reserves available to countries who were temporarily experiencing a serious shortage of foreign exchange reserves. Countries would only be asked to lend when their own balance of payments and reserves position was healthy.

The **Transport Act** of this year provided for an improved structure for the nationalised transport undertakings and gave them commercial freedom to develop their assets. The accumulated railway losses were written off to the extent of £475m. and some £650–£700m. of railway capital was exempted from fixed interest or fixed repayment obligations.

The **Road Traffic Act** provided for new and stronger measures for road safety and in particular made provision for chemical tests to determine whether a driver had been drinking alcohol. The Act directed the courts to have regard to any evidence of alcohol or drugs. Rules were laid down for disqualification of convicted offenders from holding a driving licence.

The **Pensions (Increase) Act** increased, for the fifth time since Conservatives came into office in 1951, the pensions of retired public servants such as civil servants, teachers, police and firemen. The amount of the increases varied with the greatest help going to those who had been retired the longest. Additional increases were provided for those aged over 70.

The **Health Visiting and Social Work (Training) Act** implemented one of the main recommendations of the Younghusband Report on Social Workers in the Local Authority Health and Welfare Services (May 1959) by setting up two linked training councils – the Council for the Training of Health Visitors and the Council for Training in Social Work.

The **Education Act** had two main aims – first, to give statutory authority for the improvements in the system of students grants which were announced following the report of the Anderson Committee (May 1960) and, second, to reduce the number of school-leaving dates in the year, as recommended by the Crowther Committee (August 1959).

Under the Act, awards became automatic where the student had both the necessary qualifications and a university place. The parental means test for awards was relaxed with the result that at least 10,000 more families no longer had to pay any contributions and most others were greatly helped, many to the extent of more than half the contributions which they previously paid. The number of school-leaving dates in the year were reduced from three to two.

The **Commonwealth Immigrants Act** provided for the control of immigration from the Commonwealth in a sensible and humane way in the light of the jobs and living conditions taining here. Immigration control under this Act started on 1st July 1962 and applied to the Commonwealth as a whole. But, under this Act those who were born in the UK or held passports issued by the UK government were exempt from control. The need for control had arisen because of the abnormal increase in the number of immigrants from the West Indies, Pakistan, India, and Cyprus, and to a lesser extent from Africa, Aden and Hong Kong, who were attracted by the high living standards in this country. Both the Labour and Liberal Parties in the House of Commons opposed this measure at every stage. They voted against the second and third readings of the bill and put forward amendments which, if carried, could have had the effect of allowing unrestricted immigration to continue.

The **Criminal Justice Administration Act** implemented certain recommendations made by a committee under the chairmanship of Mr Justice Streatfeild which reported in February 1961. The main aim of this act was to bring about the speedier dispatch of business by the courts in England and Wales and so reduce the waiting period before trial.

The **Licensing (Scotland) Act** was based on the recommendations of the Guest Committee which reported in November 1960. The provisions of this Act were broadly similar to those contained in the Licensing Act 1961 which applied to England and Wales after taking account of Scottish circumstances. The Act provided for uniform hours both for licensed premises and clubs, but, special provisions were made to meet the needs of sporting clubs during the winter months.

The **Housing (Scotland) Act,** like the Housing Act 1961 for England and Wales, took account of the fact that after ten years of intensive house building, housing needs differed considerably from area to area. The Act therefore gave a higher subsidy to those areas with the greatest need. But, because housing needs in Scotland were in general greater than in England and Wales, the level of subsidies under this Act was higher than south of the border.

The **Local Government (Financial Provisions, Etc.) (Scotland) Act** provided for 50 per cent mandatory relief in respect of premises occupied by charities – a provision which had already been made for England and Wales.

The Act also improved the arrangements in Scotland for determining the Exchequer General Grant to local authorities by making certain changes which had been shown to be necessary in the light of experience.

Conservative Private Members measures which reached the Statute Book during this year included:

- (*a*) The **Air Guns and Shot Guns, Etc, Act** which controlled the possession and use of air guns and shot guns by young people;
- (*b*) The **Animals (Cruel Poisons) Act** which implemented the recommendations of a Home Office Committee by giving the Home Secretary the power to designate certain poisons as 'cruel poisons' if they were cruel in operation and if alternative methods of destruction of wild animals were available. Under this Act any person using such a poison became guilty of an offence.
- (*c*) The **Landlord and Tenant Act** which required landlords in England and Wales to provide tenants with certain necessary information in connection with the letting.
- (*d*) The **Law Reform (Husband and Wife) Act** which allowed a husband and wife to take certain legal proceedings against each other.
- (*e*) The **Lotteries and Gaming Act** which provided that lotteries held for the benefit of club funds were legal and thereby restored the position to what it was thought to be before the House of Lords judgment on *Bradley* v *Payne and others* in the summer of 1961.

1963

The proposals contained in Mr Reginald Maudling's budget of this year were included in the **Finance Act.** As Mr Maudling said: 'the theme of this budget is expansion, expansion without inflation, expansion that can be sustained'. Personal tax reliefs were improved and so were the special reliefs for groups like the elderly. These improvements, taken together, completely exempted about 3,750,000 people from income tax. Considerable improvements were made in the depreciation allowances available to industry and, as Mr Maudling pointed out, as a result of these improvements the depreciation allowances available to British industry compared favourably with any of our competitors in the western world. In areas of high unemployment (development areas) industry was enabled to offset all expenditure in respect of depreciation against any tax liability. In order to encourage home ownership the rate of stamp duty on share transfers, house conveyances, mortgages and leases which had been doubled by the Socialists in 1947, was halved; many lower-priced houses were exempted from Stamp Duty altogether. Schedule A tax on owner-occupiers of residential property and on owner-occupiers of business premises and farms was abolished altogether.

The **Contracts of Employment Act** helped all employed people in two ways. First, it gave them the statutory right to a reasonable period of notice before dismissal; (after two years employment the minimum notice was two weeks and after five years four weeks). Second, employers became liable to give their employees a written statement of their employment conditions such as rates of pay, hours of work, holidays and holiday pay, sickness pay and pension rights. The Government emphasised that the Act was only the 'first stage' of their programme for improving the status and security of employees, and only laid down minimum terms upon which industry itself should build.

The **Offices, Shops and Railway Premises Act** protected the health, safety and welfare of the estimated eight million people who worked in such premises – which included about 400,000 offices, over 650,000 shops, and approximately 30,000 railway premises. Under the terms of the Act minimum standards were laid down to ensure cleanliness, reasonable temperature, ventilation, and good lighting, together with adequate seating, first-aid and washing facilities. There were also provisions dealing with fire precautions and overcrowding, and with the training and supervision of young people working with dangerous equipment.

The **Local Employment Act** provided for a fixed grant of 25 per cent of the actual cost of new buildings or extensions in areas of high unemployment (development areas) – compared with the previous ad hoc scheme under which such grants averaged 17 per cent. The Act also provided for a new fixed grant of 10 per cent of the cost of new plant and machinery – if this would create additional employment and did not merely constitute replacement. Previously only loans were available for plant and machinery.

The **Fort William Pulp and Paper Mills Act** provided the necessary finance which made it possible for Wiggins Teape and Company Limited to establish pulp and paper mills at Fort William, Inverness-shire.

The **Weights and Measures Act** completely overhauled the provisions, administration and enforcement of the law defining units of weight and measurement and the regulation of their use in trade – described by the Molony Committee as 'plainly part of the basic vocabulary of consumer protection'. Among other things this Act provided for the first time a uniform general protection against short weight, improved and extended the legal rules governing the sale of most foodstuffs and many other goods and broke new ground by covering such goods as cosmetics, soap and detergents, petrol, oil and anti-freeze.

The **Protection of Depositors Act** made it compulsory for hire purchase companies, finance companies, etc. to publicise essential information when advertising for deposits, thus giving additional protection to investors.

The **Agriculture (Miscellaneous Provisions) Act** followed the pattern of earlier Conservative legislation in helping to strengthen the economic and competitive position of the industry. In particular it enlarged both the Farm Improvement Scheme and the scheme for assisting land improvements in the hills. It provided for new schemes to grant-aid winter-keep in the hills and for the improvement of permanent grassland.

The **National Insurance Act** of this year provided for an all-round increase in benefits – the fifth improvement to take place since the Conservatives came into office in October 1951. Similar increases were made in war disability pensions by Royal Warrant. As a result of these improvements the rates of the main benefits had more than doubled since 1951 which was well ahead of the increase in prices. In December of this year further improvements were made in the provision for widows with children. First, the widowed mothers' personal allowance was enabled to continue until the last child's nineteenth birthday instead of 18 as formerly. Second, widowed mothers became able to draw family allowances and child allowances up to the child's nineteenth birthday if he was in full-time education or apprenticeship.

The **Children and Young Persons Act** laid a duty on local authorities in Britain to make advice, guidance and assistance available to families where the need arose, the aim being to keep the family together and so avoid a situation where the children had to be taken into public care or brought before the court. The Act also provided that the child victim or witness of a sexual offence in England and Wales would not normally have to give oral evidence at the committal stage in the Magistrates' Court; evidence could be given by means of a written statement. Other provisions in this Act included a simpler form of oath for children in Magistrates' Courts in England and Wales, and the raising of the maximum fine for cruelty to children on summary conviction in England and Wales. The Act made it clear that the attendance of both parents of a child offender at court might be required unless it was unreasonable to do so. The Act also raised from 15 to 16 the age limit under which a child in Britain might normally take part without licence in entertainment where an admission charge was made to the audience.

The **Public Order Act** substantially increased the penalties for offensive words or behaviour in public places or at public meetings leading to a breach of the peace. The penalties went up from £50 or three months imprisonment (or both) to £100 or three months imprisonment (or both) on summary conviction, or £500 or one year (or both) on indictment.

The **Water Resources Act** provided for new river authorities to be responsible for the management of water resources in each river basin in England and Wales, together with a new central body to co-ordinate on a national scale the conservation activities of the various new river authorities. The new central authority became called the Water Resources Board.

The **London Government Act** reformed the structure of local government in the Greater London Area. It established thirty-two new London boroughs as the main units of local administration in London carrying responsibility for the important personal social services. The Act also set up a directly elected Greater London Council in place of the former London County Council for the purpose of carrying out functions which needed to be planned over Greater London as a whole. Under the Act education became the responsibility of the newly created London boroughs except for a central area where it was administered by an Inner London Education Authority; it was intended that these arrangements under this Act for the central area were to be the subject of a review before 1970.

The **Television Act** contained three main provisions. First, it strengthened the powers of the Independent Television Authority (ITA), as regards maintenance of standards and balance of programmes; provision was made for the drawing up of a code of standards. Second, it gave the ITA improved powers to prevent a dominance of the television network by the large programme companies. Third, it provided for the programme companies to make a special payment to the Exchequer based on advertising receipts in the light of the very large profits which the companies had been making. This new payment replaced the Television Advertisements Duty provided for in the Finance Act of 1961.

The **Education (Scotland) Act** provided for the establishment of a Board to conduct the Scottish Certificate of Education Examinations and improved the Scottish teachers' superannuation scheme. It enabled teachers to become non-elected members of their local council's education committee and allowed salary increases to be back-dated to the date on which the recommendation for the increase was received by the Secretary of State.

The **Criminal Justice (Scotland) Act** made similar provision in

Scotland to that provided for in England and Wales by the Criminal Justice Act 1961. It provided for the establishment of new institutions known as young offenders institutions for those between the ages of 17 and 21, to give training geared to their needs, instead of their being sent to prison to mix with hardened criminals. Compulsory after-care was extended to inmates of detention centres and the new young offenders institutions and to various groups of older prisoners. Provision was made for a statutory scheme of legal aid in criminal cases to replace informal arrangements.

Conservative Private Members measures included:
(1) The **Animal Boarding Establishments Act** which provided that keepers of animal boarding establishments in Britain must be licensed by a local authority, and that they must ensure suitable heating, cleanliness, ventilation, and isolation in event of diseases, etc.
(2) The **Deer Act,** which provided for a close season for deer in England and Wales and prohibited the use of small rifles or airguns to kill deer.

1964

The proposals of Mr Reginald Maudling's second budget were embodied in the **Finance Act** of this year. Mr Maudling said that the purpose of this budget was broadly the same as that of his first budget in April 1963, namely to achieve expansion without inflation. As **Mr Maudling** said: 'Although last year's budget was described as timid and cautious (by Mr Jay and Mr Callaghan) it has been followed by an expansion at the annual rate of at least 5 per cent in total production and a fall of over 150,000 in unemployment. Trade is buoyant; business confidence is high; investment in industry is gathering pace.'

Mr George Woodcock, then General Secretary of the TUC said: 'I am bound to say that this is a budget of considerable courage.' (Television Interview, 14th April 1964) Special tax reliefs for the elderly were improved. But, there were increases in the taxes on alcohol and tobacco in order to prevent inflation without harming industrial modernisation and economic growth.

The **Industrial Training Act** had three main aims: first, to secure an adequate amount of training in industry at all levels of employment; second, to improve the quality of training given; and third, to secure as far as possible an equitable distribution of the costs of training. By the end of 1969, twenty-eight industrial training boards had been set up, covering an estimated total of about sixteen million workers, or 86 per cent of the labour force covered by the Act.

The **Resale Prices Act** which is associated with Mr Edward Heath, then Secretary of State for Industry, Trade and Regional Development, was designed to end the practice known as 'resale price maintenance'. Accordingly, it provided that, except for exempted goods, suppliers could not fix minimum retail prices, or withhold supplies because a retailer cut prices; but they could withhold goods if the retailer was using them as 'loss leaders' – i.e. not to make a profit but to attract custom (seasonal and clearance sales were not affected). Provision was made for suppliers continuing resale price maintenance to notify the Registrar of Restrictive Trading Agreements. It was provided that resale price maintenance could continue for the goods registered until the Restrictive Practices Court reached a decision. To gain exemption the parties had to show, first that if RPM was ended customers would suffer detriment, and second, that the detriment would out-weigh any disadvantage resulting from the continuance of RPM. As a result of this Act a wide range of items were reduced in price including chocolates and sweets, petrol, light fittings, razor blades, paint, wallpaper, sewing machines, nylon and nylon clothing, sports goods and a variety of electrical goods.

The **Shipbuilding Credit Act** gave effect to the Government Shipbuilding Credit Scheme, under which loans of up to £75m. were made to British shipowners placing orders in British shipyards. The individual loans, available in suitable cases for up to 80 per cent of the cost of the ship, could be made for periods of up to a maximum of ten years at the then current government lending rate and were repayable by instalments. (The loan scheme was temporary and expired in March 1964, by which time the whole of the £75m. had been taken up.)

The **Shipping Contracts and Commercial Documents Act** protected British interests by ensuring that the Government could prohibit British shipowners from complying with demands of any foreign country for the disclosure of commercial documents or information. The Act was made necessary by the actions of the United States Federal Maritime Commission particularly in issuing orders that British shipowners and traders should break their 'dual freight rate' contracts and sign new ones in a form to be laid down by the American government, and by their demand that foreign shipping lines should disclose certain information relating to freight rates located in and outside the United States. The British government at once made it clear that it regarded this American demand as a trespass of UK jurisdiction and this Act gave statutory effect to this policy.

The **Harbours Act** put into effect the main recommendations of the Report of the Rochdale Committee on the major ports of Great Britain (September 1962). The Act established a National Ports Council to formulate plans for the improvement of existing, and the provision of new, harbours in Great Britain and all services and facilities provided at such harbours. It also provided for the control of harbour development and for financial assistance for the improvement of harbours.

The **Hire-Purchase Act** largely implemented the recommendations of the Molony Committee on Consumer Protection. First, this Act added to the basic safeguards in the Hire-Purchase Act, 1938 (which gave a hirer important rights and required that these should be clearly stated in the agreement) and extended this to cover all agreements (other than those where the hirer was a body corporate) involving a total hire-purchase price of up to £2,000 (instead of the previous limits of £300 in general and £1,000 for livestock). Second, this Act gave a new safeguard against the less reputable type of doorstep salesman by providing for a four-day 'cooling off' period during which the hirer could cancel an agreement signed anywhere but in 'appropriate trade premises'.

The **Agriculture and Horticulture Act** substantially increased aid to the horticulture industry with the aim of reducing production costs and improving marketing. The Act provided for a new horticulture improvement scheme and greatly extended the range of equipment eligible for grant.

The **Family Allowances and National Insurance Act** provided more help for widows with children to look after by increasing the rates of National Insurance child benefit and Family Allowances which they could receive. In addition the Act

(*a*) raised the amounts which pensioners and widowed mothers could earn without loss of pension or benefit and

(*b*) enabled family allowances and national insurance child dependency benefits to be drawn up to the age of 19 where the child was either at school or a full-time pupil at college or an apprentice.

The **Education Act** gave local education authorities and voluntary bodies in England and Wales more freedom to experiment with the age of transfer from primary to secondary schools. Previously all children had to be transferred from primary to secondary schools between the ages of 10 and 12½. But this Act enabled local authorities to establish new schools with an age range of 9–13.

The **Housing Act** provided for the setting up of a Housing Corporation with up to £100m. Exchequer finance to stimulate building of homes by housing societies for renting or co-ownership without profit or subsidy, and gave building societies new powers to lend to housing societies. The Act also improved the arrangements governing entitlement to the standard grants for certain basic amenities and gave local authorities stronger powers to protect tenants in multi-occupied houses against exploitation.

The **Police Act** improved the organisation of police forces in

England and Wales by giving the Home Secretary a general duty to promote police efficiency and provided him with new powers for this purpose, and increased substantially the maximum penalties for assaulting or obstructing a police constable.

The **Malicious Damage Act** greatly increased both the maximum fine for malicious damage to property which could be imposed by Magistrates' Courts and the amount of compensation which offenders could be ordered to pay by the court.

The **Drugs (Prevention of Misuse) Act** dealt with the problem of 'pep pills', such as 'purple hearts', by making it an offence to possess them except on a doctor's prescription.

The **Obscene Publications Act** strengthened the law against obscene publications by making possession of an obscene article an offence as well as its publication.

The **Refreshment Houses Act** dealt with the problem of 'clip-joints' by giving stronger powers to authorities which licensed establishments serving refreshments between 10 p.m. and 5 a.m.

The **Criminal Appeal Act** conferred on the Court of Criminal Appeal power to order a new trial in certain circumstances.

Conservative Private Members measures included:

(1) The **Hairdressers (Registration) Act** which was designed to promote proper standards of competence in hairdressing by providing for the registration of hairdressers.

(2) The **Young Persons (Employment) Act** which prevented young people under 18 years of age from being employed in night clubs, etc.

(3) The **Trade Union (Amalgamations Etc.) Act** which facilitated the amalgamation or merger of trade unions where this was desired by the majority of the members concerned.

(4) The **Protection of Animals (Anaesthetics) Act** which enlarged the classes of operations on animals in which anaesthetics must be used.

PART THREE

The early 1970s
1970 to 1974

A CONSERVATIVE GOVERNMENT with Mr Edward Heath as Prime Minister came into office following the General Election of June 1970. It remained in office until the General Election of February 1974. This period of nearly four years of Conservative government saw considerable simplification of the whole tax system and significant improvements in the social services, such as the care of the elderly and the disabled, and education, with a much greater concentration of resources on meeting urgent social needs many of which – for example the needs of the mentally ill and the mentally handicapped – had been neglected in the past.

As is invariably the case the legacy inherited from Labour in June 1970 was one of failure.

The legacy inherited from Labour

The period of Labour government between 1964/70 was unhappily one of little or no economic growth, rising unemployment, the worst wage and price inflation for twenty years, big tax increases and a heavy burden of debt with the short and long term debts incurred by the Labour government standing at £1,500m. by June 1970.

Economic growth

The rate of economic growth averaged 2.3 per cent a year which meant that the economy expanded a third less fast than the 25 per cent growth achieved over the previous six Conservative years. This slowing down cost the country over £12,000m. of potential wealth – about £750 for every family in the land. Production in industry was actually slower in June 1970 than it had been a year earlier.

Unemployment

The number of people out of work more than doubled in the last four years under Labour. It exceeded half a million in 35 out of the 42 months between the beginning of 1967 and June 1970 as compared with in only 8 months during the whole thirteen years of Conservative government between 1951 and 1964.

The standard of living

The standard of living as measured by after-tax income per head of population, adjusted for price increases rose by only one-third as fast under Labour as in the previous five years of Conservative government. It rose by only 1 per cent a year instead of 3 per cent a year. As the Child Poverty Action Group pointed out, low income families were relatively worse off after six years of Labour government because the gap between average earnings and the average wage paid to those on the lowest level of earnings widened.

Taxation

The annual tax burden was raised by £3,000m. a year which was equivalent to £3.50 a week for every family in the land. Four new taxes were introduced including Selective Employment Tax – and almost all others were raised.

Wage and price inflation

When Labour left office the rate of wage and price inflation was the worst for twenty years. Wage increases had been far outstripping increases in productivity.

Pensions and social welfare

The failure to achieve economic growth resulted in a disappointing rate of progress in the improvement of social services. Under Labour the real value of the retirement pension increased by an average of 2½ per cent a year as compared with 4 per cent during the thirteen years of Conservative government.

Under the Labour government the hospital building programme went up by an average of 10 per cent a year in real terms compared with an average increase in real terms of 25 per cent a year in the last three years of the previous Conservative government.

Progress in dealing with out-dated schools was much slower than under the previous Conservative government and although Labour promised to increase the provision made for day release the number of workers on day release in 1968–1969 was fewer than four years previously.

Housing

Labour inherited a rising house building programme when they came into office in October 1974, but, when they left office in June 1970, the house building programme had fallen below the levels of 1964 and was steadily declining.

Summary of progress June 1970 to February 1974

THE PERIOD June 1970 to February 1974 saw a record progress in reducing taxation, a major increase in our standard of living generally and considerable progress in improving the social services particularly in the case of the most urgent social needs such as the care of the very old, the chronically disabled, poorer families, and in dealing with outdated hospitals and schools.

In December 1973, following the energy crisis, Mr Barber announced a number of economies over the whole field of public spending to take effect in the next financial year (1974/75). If the incoming Labour government had followed this prudent and sensible move, our general economic circumstances, and in particular the position as regards prices and jobs, would today be a good deal healthier than is the case. But instead the Labour government doubled public spending and as a result the number of jobless has doubled and the income tax burden has more than doubled. In 1973/74 under the Conservatives the average income tax burden per household was £389 a year but in 1976/77 it was estimated at £869 a year. Britain has suffered – and is still suffering – from the worst inflation in British history – much worse than in most other Western countries.

The main highlights of progress under the Conservatives during the period June 1970 to February 1974 are summarised below.

Growth of the economy

The Conservatives achieved a much faster rate of economic growth than the previous Labour government and as a result it was possible to reduce considerably the burden of taxation and at the same time to improve the social services. By 1973 the economy was expanding at the rate of 5 per cent a year which was twice as fast as under the previous Labour government.

Prices and incomes

Between June 1970 and January 1974 prices rose by nearly 37 per cent which compares with an increase of 155 per cent in world commodity prices over the same period. Thus, under the Conservatives, prices rose only one-quarter as fast as world prices.

In contrast, under the previous Labour government prices in Britain rose twice as fast as world prices.

What is most significant is that the standard of living per head of the British people (i.e. what people's net incomes will actually buy) rose more in three Conservative years (13 per cent) than in the whole of Labour's six years of office (8½ per cent).

Taxation

Between June 1970 and February 1974 the yearly burden of taxes was cut by £4,000m. In other words if Labour's tax rates had still been in force in February 1974 when the Conservatives left office, the British people would have been paying well over £4,000m. more in taxation than they actually were. The income tax burden alone was reduced by at least £1.50 a week on average for every family in Britain. This reduction of about £4,000m. in the yearly tax burden under the Conservatives compares with an increase of some £3,000m. in the yearly tax burden under the 1964/70 Labour government.

The cut in the burden of income tax over this period was the largest ever made in any comparable period in history. The cut in indirect taxation, that is to say taxes on spending, amounted to a total of some £900m. A cut of about £1,000m. was made in the annual burden of tax on industry.

Pensions and benefits

These were increased three times, and as a result their buying power went up by more in three years of Conservative government than it did in the previous six years under Labour. In addition, six new cash benefits were introduced which helped some two million people in need, such as the over-80s, the chronic sick, the very seriously disabled, widows who previously got no pension at all and low wage earning families with children. The previous Labour government had introduced no new cash benefits.

The Conservatives had longer term plans which were designed greatly to reduce dependence on means-tested benefits, particularly in the case of old people. First, the Social Security Act 1973 provided that over the years all employed people would get a good earnings-related pension on top of the basic state pension either from occupational schemes or, where this was not possible, from a reserve state scheme. Second, in 1972 proposals were published for a tax credit scheme which, as well as greatly simplifying the tax and social security systems, would have provided more help automatically without the need for individual application and means-testing for old people and poorer families.

Education

There was considerable expansion in all sectors of education, with priority given to primary school improvements because these schools were often housed in the most outdated buildings. Under a record programme for dealing with primary schools, improvements in about

1,000 outdated schools had either been or were being dealt with by the time Conservatives left office.

The school building programme for the first three years of Conservative government was in real terms about £240m. greater than in the previous three years under Labour. Mrs Thatcher's 1972 White Paper entitled 'A Framework for Expansion' outlined targets for continuing expansion in education. Under the proposals in this White Paper, major programmes were launched for the expansion of nursery education, for improvements in both the training and supply of teachers, and in the provision made for the education of handicapped children.

Health and welfare

A higher priority than ever before was given to these services. As a result, there was a major expansion in the home-help service, an increase of over 30,000 in the number of nurses in the first two years of Conservative government and the launching of a major hospital building programme far in excess of anything previously achieved by Labour. Sir Keith Joseph, Conservative Secretary of State for the Social Services ensured that for the first time a real priority was given to the needs of previously neglected groups like the mentally ill and the mentally handicapped. The late Mr Richard Crossman, former Labour Secretary of State for the Social Services, paid a generous tribute to what Sir Keith Joseph had done in improving the long stay hospitals for the mentally ill or handicapped, when he said:

> 'he (Sir Keith Joseph) shared my sense of outrage at the scandal of the long stay hospitals – and has also been more successful than I was at extracting from the Treasury the funds necessary to put these scandals right.' (*The Times*, 9th August 1972)

Housing

The number of new houses or older houses for which modernisation grants were approved totalled about two million in the Conservative government's first three years, more than half a million more than in the previous three years of Labour government. Tenants in need, whether living in council houses or privately rented homes, furnished or unfurnished, were able to get generous help with the rent, and as a result a record number of two million people benefited.

Home ownership was made possible for the first time for over a million people in the first three Conservative years. About half these families were on average male industrial earnings or less.

There was a considerable increase in the number of families buying their council homes; for example, in 1972 nine times as many families bought their council homes as in 1970.

The subsidy system was recast to concentrate help on areas and people in need and the aim of the Housing and Planning Bill, which failed to reach the statute book because of the intervention of the February 1974 General Election, was to deal with the remaining black spots of housing squalor; most of the provisions of this bill were subsequently re-enacted by the Labour government.

The environment

A major drive was launched to provide cleaner air, cleaner rivers and an improved environment in general. Under the Conservatives about 2½ miles of polluted rivers were being cleansed every week. Air pollution was reduced, letting more sun into our cities than at any time for 150 years. Derelict land was being restored rapidly with a total of 13,000 acres cleared since 1970.

The Protection of the Environment Bill, which did not reach the statute book because of the intervention of the February General Election had the aim of spearheading a new drive to deal with air pollution and the problem of nuisance caused by noise. Most of the provisions of this bill were subsequently re-enacted by legislation introduced by Labour.

1970

Although a Conservative government was in office only for the second half of this year, a number of important Conservative Acts reached the statute book before the end of 1970.

The **National Insurance Act** provided three new social security cash benefits.

- (*a*) A special pension known as the Old Persons pension to be payable as of right without a means test to all those who did not qualify for the retirement pension because they were too old to come into the National Insurance scheme when it started in July 1948. This special pension (which became payable from November of this year) benefited about 110,000 old people aged 80 or over.

- (*b*) A pension on a sliding scale according to the age at which widowhood had taken place for those women widowed between the ages of 40 and 50 who previously got no permanent pension. This sliding scale pension which started in April 1971 benefited immediately nearly 100,000 widows, but, of course, the numbers qualifying for it increased over the years.

- (*c*) A special tax-free allowance known as the attendance allowance to be paid to those very seriously disabled people, irrespective of age, who needed a good deal of attention both day and night. This allowance started in December 1971 and by mid-1973 was benefiting about 95,000 very seriously disabled people. In June 1973 this allowance was extended at a lower rate to those seriously disabled people who required a good deal of attention day *or* night. By April 1976 the number qualifying for the allowance had reached about 230,000.

A number of Conservatives, notably Mr Airey Neave, now a member of Mrs Thatcher's Shadow Cabinet, had introduced Private Members Bills during the period of the 1964-1970 Labour Government to provide pensions for the over-80's but all these measures were blocked by Labour.

The **Family Income Supplements Act** provided for a new benefit – the Family Income Supplement – (FIS) – which started in August 1971 and became payable to low wage earning families in full time work with children. This scheme lays down certain prescribed amounts which vary according to the size of family and what families actually receive is one-half of the amount by which their gross incomes fall short of these prescribed amounts. By 1975 about 60,000 families were drawing family income supplement. The Labour Party voted against this measure, but since being returned to office following the February 1974 General Election they have continued to use the scheme. This scheme was intended as a means of bringing immediate help to low wage earning families pending more comprehensive arrangements for tackling family poverty such as those which were later envisaged under the 1972 Conservative proposals for tax credits.

In the field of education, one of the earliest steps taken by the Conservative government on its return to office was to issue on 30th June 1970, a circular 10/70 which withdrew previous Labour government circulars to local education authorities, under which they were expected to submit plans for reorganising secondary education on completely comprehensive lines. Thus local education authorities were left free to decide for themselves whether or not to prepare reorganisation schemes covering all or some of the schools for which they were responsible. Under Labour local education authorities had been asked to submit schemes for turning all their secondary schools into comprehensives, and legislation had been introduced to make this compulsory, although it failed to reach the statute book before the 1970 General Election.

The **Education (Handicapped Children) Act** provided that the responsibility for the education of mentally handicapped children would be transferred from local health authorities to local education authorities. As a result the needs of some 30,000 mentally handicapped children then in training centres, hospitals for the mentally handicapped and special care units for children with serious physical disabilities or behaviour disorders were for the first time considered along with those of the 100,000 children then in special schools for the handicapped. Later in November 1973 Mrs Margaret Thatcher (then Secretary of State for Education and Science) announced an enquiry into the education of handicapped children under the Chairmanship of Professor Mary Warnock. Mrs Thatcher's 1972 White Paper, 'A Framework for Expansion', provided for an expanded building programme of special schools.

The **Harbours (Amendment) Act** enabled the Government to continue to provide financial assistance for harbour development under the 1964 Conservative government's Harbours Act; this Act was necessary because the limit of assistance fixed under the 1964 Act had been reached.

1971

The proposals in Mr Anthony (now Lord) Barber's first budget were embodied in the **Finance Act** of this year. In Mr Barber's words, the purpose of this budget was to 'herald a new approach, an approach based on the belief that lower taxation and simpler taxation will, over the years ahead, help to create a new spirit – a new spirit of personal endeavour and achievement which alone can provide our nation with growing prosperity'. The budget, therefore, concentrated on restoring incentives, encouraging savings, lightening the heavy hand of government and paving the way for a faster growth in living standards. The main provisions of this budget were

   (*i*) a reduction of 2½p in the standard rate of income tax; this proposal had been announced by Mr Barber in October 1970;
   (*ii*) improvements in the various special tax allowances for the elderly and those looking after dependant relatives;
   (*iii*) corporation tax, which had been reduced from 45 per cent to 42½ per cent in October 1970, was reduced further to 40 per cent by this budget;
   (*iv*) improved capital allowances for machinery and plant were provided for and free depreciation for investment in industrial plant and machinery in areas of high unemployment was introduced;
   (*v*) the rate of selective employment tax (SET) was halved;
   (*vi*) stamp duty on mortgages was abolished;
   (*vii*) capital gains tax was eased and estate duty was reduced in order to exempt more small estates.

Labour's legislation aggregating a child's income with that of its parents for tax purposes ceased to have effect and married women were enabled to have their earned incomes assessed as single persons for tax purposes instead of being aggregated with their husbands; (where wives take up this option, the husbands are assessed as single persons on the remaining joint income.) This provision put right an anomaly whereby in some cases it was more profitable for a couple to live together than to get married.

Later in July 1971 all rates of purchase tax were reduced and hire purchase restrictions were abolished.

In order to find the money for these tax reductions and improved incentives for industry, Mr Barber carried out a long-overdue review of public spending. As a result the Government were enabled to adopt new priorities in public spending which meant more help for people and services genuinely in need, but at the same time those who could afford it paid more for things like school meals and use of the health service.

The **Investment and Building Grants Act** carried a stage further the Government's aim of encouraging profitability in industry and the improvement in the quality of investment. This sensible strategy replaced Labour's policy of combining high taxation with indiscriminate grants – a self-defeating process. The budget had already reduced corporation tax and introduced improved capital allowances. This Act ended Labour's indiscriminate investment grants for plant and machinery in areas of high unemployment. Labour's totally indiscriminate and wasteful system of investment grants suffered from three specific disadvantages:

(i) The investment grants benefited firms regardless of whether the firms were making profits;

(ii) Labour's system discriminated unjustifiably against the service industries;

(iii) The detailed information required to support claims for grants imposed a considerable administrative burden and cost on industry.

Under this new Act part of the savings resulting from the abolition of the former investment grants were used to improve the building grants available in the areas of high unemployment. In total – the new incentives reduced corporation tax, improved capital allowances and improved building grants; they were the most powerful since the War and they gave considerably more help to areas of high unemployment. The discrimination against the service industries which obtained under the old system was ended.

The **Coal Industry Act** empowered the Government to 'hive-off' activities which were not central to the functions of the National Coal Board; either by sale or in partnership with private enterprise.

The **Atomic Energy Act** authorised the transfer of fuel production from the state-owned Atomic Energy Authority to British Nuclear Fuels Limited, and of isotope production to the Radiochemical Centre Limited, thus enabling private enterprise undertakings to participate in these activities.

The **Civil Aviation Act** established the Civil Aviation Authority to regulate the British civil aviation industry as a whole including safety and licensing, and created a British Airways Board charged with overall management of the public sector airlines.

The **Industry Act** abolished the Industrial Reorganisation Corporation established under Labour's Industrial Reorganisation Act 1966; Conservatives had criticised the IRC as being an unnecessary body adding to bureaucracy and more of an hindrance than a help to industry. The Act also provided for the winding up of the investment allowances to industry to co-incide with the starting of the new Conservative investment scheme.

The **Rolls Royce Purchase Act** authorised the purchase by the Government of the aero-engine divisions essential to British joint defence projects, because of the imminent bankruptcy of this company.

The **Mineral Workings (Offshore Installations) Act** made provision for the safety, health and welfare of persons on offshore drilling installations and for the safety of such installations and the operations carried out on or near them.

The **Industrial Relations Act** created a framework for industrial relations. It established employees' rights to join a trade union, to compensation for unfair dismissal, unions' right to recognition, information and agency shop agreements. It set out the right to strike, created the presumption that collective agreements were intended to be legally enforceable unless they stated otherwise, set up the National Industrial Relations Court and Registrar of Trades Unions and Employers' Organisations, and provided emergency powers to impose cooling off periods or strike ballots in emergency situations.

Although this Act has since been repealed by Labour, some of its provisions strengthening the rights of employees, for example, as regards protection against unfair dismissal, were re-enacted.

The **Merchant Shipping (Oil Pollution) Act** dealt with liability and compensation where oil pollution occurred at sea, and made the owner of the ship from which oil escaped liable for any damage caused in the area of the UK and for the cost of any remedial measures. It also required ships carrying more than 2,000 tons of oil to be compulsorily insured against liability.

The **Oil in Navigable Waters Act** strengthened the provisions for preventing pollution of the sea by oil, and imposed a fine of £50,000 for certain offences on summary conviction.

The **Housing Act** increased the amount of financial assistance available to local authorities over the next three years for the improvement of older houses in areas where improvement was badly needed, but had been lagging. It provided for a £46m. boost to modernise the massive stock of older houses in these areas. This scheme was a great success and was extended for a further year by legislation passed in 1973.

The **Land Commission (Dissolution) Act** abolished the betterment levy and provided for the dissolution of the Land Commission set up under the Land Commission Act 1967. As Conservatives had consistently forecast would happen, the chief sufferers from the betterment levy had been widows and families of limited means and not the big land speculators.

The **Rating Act** made it clear that all buildings which a farmer used for the purposes of his farm were exempt from rates. Because of technical and scientific advances in farming, farm buildings used for intensive livestock rearing had become liable for rates contrary to the original intention of Parliament.

The **Highways Act** improved road construction procedure and made better arrangements for considering objections to proposed highway schemes in England and Wales.

The **Water Resources Act** gave improved powers to river authorities in England and Wales to carry out water schemes and laid down procedures for holding local public inquiries.

The **National Insurance Act** authorised, from September 1971, major increases in pensions and other social insurance benefits, and over and above this gave extra cash help to pensioners over 80, and those chronic sick wage earners and their families, who had been unable to work for at least six months due to illness. The provision of this extra help for priority groups under this Act was a continuation of the policy pursued by the previous Conservative government when, under legislation passed in 1956, extra help by way of specially high national insurance child dependants' allowances were provided for widows with children to look after and the third and subsequent children of a family became entitled to a higher family allowance than that paid for a second child. The special help provided under the 1971 Act for the chronically sick took the form of a new invalidity allowance payable over and above normal sickness benefit renamed 'invalidity pension' and about half a million chronically sick wage earners were given extra help in this way. Additional help for the over 80s took the form of a special addition paid over and above the normal retirement or special over-80s pension and this helped about 1,250,000 very old people.

The **Social Security Act** tightened up the rules governing the payment of supplementary benefit to families of men on strike and ended the payment of benefits for the first three days of sickness, unemployment or injury benefit.

The **Pensions (Increase) Act** improved public service pensions, provided for these pensions to be reviewed every two years and lowered the age at which increases could be paid from 60 to 55.

The **Immigration Act** gave the most effective and far-reaching control over immigration that any government has ever had. This Act provided that in future immigrants coming here to work could obtain work permits entitling them to stay in Britain for a temporary period only (normally a year), to work at a specific job, in a specific place; these work permits replaced the former employment vouchers which enabled people with certain skills to come here under a quota system for permanent settlement and look for a job. The Act also strengthened the law against illegal immigration and provided for a voluntary repatriation scheme under which financial assistance can be given to those wanting to return to their country of origin. According to the official statistics the effect of this Act was to reduce the number of Commonwealth immigrants coming to Britian in 1973 (the first full year of the Act's operation) to 34,044 (mostly wives and children of men already here or United Kingdom passport holders for whom Britain has a special responsibility because they have no other nationality) as compared with an average of 63,000 a year in the last three years of the 1964–1970 Labour government. Unhappily in recent years there has been an increase in immigration because the present Labour government has deliberately relaxed immigration controls.

Both the Labour and Liberal Parties in the House of Commons voted against the 1971 Act.

The **Criminal Damage Act** closely followed the recommendations of the Law Commission by simplfying the legal code governing offences involving criminal damage and rationalising the penalties for such offences. It also widened the powers of the courts to require offenders found guilty of criminally damaging property to compensate their victims.

The **Hijacking Act** enabled the United Kingdom to ratify the Convention for the Suppression of Unlawful Seizure of Aircraft which was opened for signature at The Hague on 16th December 1970.

The **Fire Precautions Act** strengthened the Law's provision relating to fire precautions where hazards to life are concerned. A system of 'fire certificates' was introduced for certain places which were outside the scope of the Factories Act 1961 and the Offices, Shops and Railway Premises Act 1963. These included places of public amusement and residential premises such as hotels, boarding houses and very high blocks of flats where people could be specially at risk.

The **Misuse of Drugs Act** distinguished between the unlawful possession of drugs and trafficking in drugs with the penalties for the latter made much more severe. In addition the Act gave the Home Secretary power to bring quickly under control any new drug which constituted a potential danger whereas under earlier legislation Britain could not act on a narcotic drug in advance of the United Nations Commission on Narcotic Drugs. It also enabled the Home Secretary to deal with practitioners who prescribed controlled drugs irresponsibly.

Scottish legislation included:

(a) The **Education (Scotland) Act** which restored to Local Authorities in Scotland the power (which had been taken away by Labour) to charge fees if they wished to do so in a limited number of their schools, and

(b) The **Hospital Endowment (Scotland) Act** which established the Scottish Hospital Trust for the purpose of administering endowments received by Scottish hospitals before the 5th November 1946 other than those transferred to the Scottish Hospital Endowments Research Trust.

Conservative Private Members legislation which reached the statute book included:

(1) The **Carriage of Goods by Sea Act** which gave effect to the relevant Hague Rules concerning sea-worthiness, bills of lading, etc. contained in the protocol agreed in Brussels in 1968.

(2) The **Consumer Protection Act** which enabled local authorities to prosecute manufacturers or importers and not only retailers where offences are committed.

(3) The **Unsolicited Goods and Services Act** which provided greater protection for persons receiving unsolicited goods and services including entries in directories.

(4) The **Motor Vehicles (Passenger Insurance) Act** which required users of motor vehicles to be insured in respect of liability for death or bodily injury to passengers.

1972

The **Finance Act** of this year embodied the proposals contained in Mr Barber's second budget. The main aim of this budget was to reduce the overall tax burden on the British people. As a result some £1,200m. was cut off tax rates in 1972/3. The main provision was an increase in the personal tax allowances which took 2,750,000 people out of the tax net altogether and reduced everyone else's tax bill by an average of more than one pound a week. This budget also dealt with a hardship often caused to widows who found that they had to sell the matrimonial home in order to meet their liability for estate duty. Under this budget, assets up to £30,000 were exempt from estate duty where left to a surviving spouse. In addition, reductions were made in estate duty, which were specifically designed to help farmers and small businesses. There were also reductions in purchase tax, but particularly important for industry was a new programme of incentives which included nationwide 100 per cent depreciation allowances with additional measures to help areas of high unemployment, subsequently embodied in the Industry Act of this year. This budget, which reduced taxation by the largest amount ever, fulfilled all the main criteria for a Conservative budget; it operated on the side of lower prices; it gave direct help to the ordinary taxpayer; it was reforming; and it was expansionary. In addition, this year saw the repayment of all outstanding post war credits.

But the most significant event in the field of taxation was the publication of proposals for a tax credit scheme. Such a scheme has many advantages, one of the most important of which is that it would enable more help to be provided automatically, without the need for individual application and means-testing, to poorer families. Tax credits would replace the existing personal tax allowances and cash family allowances. As a result the full benefit of the existing personal tax allowances would be extended, in the form of credits, to those who at present pay little or no income tax and therefore gain only marginally or not at all from these tax allowances. The scheme would therefore reduce dependence on means-testing and ensure that everyone received the help to which they were genuinely entitled; at present large numbers of people do not apply for the help to which they are entitled. At the same time the scheme would increase both the incentive to work and to earn more, thereby remedying the present thoroughly indefensible situation under which more and more families find that they have little or no incentive to increase their earnings or, indeed, to work at all.

The **Industry Act** followed a budget which had given the greatest-ever stimulus to industry with free depreciation allowances for plant and machinery and 40 per cent additional allowances for industrial buildings all over the country. As a result the main regional differentials had disappeared and the purpose of the Industry Act was to re-establish these differentials giving the areas with above average unemployment a more clear cut preference than ever before. Under this Act new regional development cash grants were made available for new or adaptation of existing buildings and new plant or machinery in areas of above average unemployment. In the words of **Mr Patrick Jenkin,** then Chief Secretary to the Treasury, 'the combined effect of nation-wide free depreciation and regional cash grants is far more profit-related than was the old pre-1970 grant system. Their combined value is worth about three times as much, on a discounted basis, to a development area firm which is profitable than to one which is unprofitable. Labour's grant subsidised both indiscriminately.' (*Hansard*, 22nd March, Col 1644)

The **Employment Medical Advisory Service Act** opened up a new era in the health care of people at work, by providing for the establishment of a new medical service. This Act replaced the part-time Family Doctor Service, and the obligatory routine medical examination of all young people in factories with a new Employment

Medical Advisory Service. The function of this service is to study and advise on effects of particular jobs on health; precautions for work with dangerous substances; medical requirements for different types of work and problems of the disabled. Doctors were empowered to require an employer to allow them to examine any employee (with his consent) whose health may be in danger at work. They have special responsibility for young people at work, for advising parents, careers officers etc, and following up young people identified at school as being in need of medical advice in relation to their work. This Act also requires that an employer engaging a young person to work in a factory must notify the local careers officer within seven days giving particulars of the work concerned.

The **Counter-Inflation (Temporary Provisions) Act** empowered the Government to apply a standstill for 90 days (extendable for a further 60 days) to prices, charges, pay, dividends and rents by forbidding any increase above the level prevailing before 6th November 1972. In November Mr Heath justified the need for this Act on the grounds that the tripartite discussions between the Government, the TUC and the CBI had broken down and there was therefore no hope for the time being of a voluntary policy of wage restraint. **Mr Heath** went on to express the hope that discussions would be resumed so that the need for this legislation would be temporary. (*Hansard*, 6th November 1972, Col 627.) The Government made no secret of their intense dislike of statutory controls, nor of their anxiety to return to normal bargaining processes as soon as possible. The Government's view was that in the absence of voluntary agreement the powers provided under this Act were necessary to prevent uncontrolled inflation. However, it was felt that in the longer term the prospects for succesful voluntary restraint in a period of good economic growth, and with provision for continued improvement in real incomes, were far better than they had ever been under the previous Labour government.

The **Harbours (Loans) Act** made loans available to assist certain port authorities which, although viable in the long term, experience difficulties in raising funds on the market for renewal of capital debt.

The **Housing Finance Act** recast the housing subsidies in England and Wales in order to concentrate them on areas and people most in need. Previous Conservative Governments had made the subsidies system much more sensible by concentrating help on urgent housing needs but under Labour's Housing Subsidies Act 1967, there had been a return to an indiscriminate and open-ended system of subsidies. What the 1972 Conservative Act did was to end indiscriminate subsidies and instead to give more help to areas with urgent housing needs and insufficient financial resources to meet these needs. At the same time it provided help with the rent to all families in need in the form of rent rebates for council house tenants and rent allowances for those living in unfurnished privately rented homes. The fair rents system which the previous Labour government had introduced for privately rented unfurnished accommodation was extended to council housing so that all families were treated in the same way. As a result of this Act some two million families got help with the rent. When the previous Labour government introduced the fair rent system for privately rented homes they provided no form of help with the rent for families in need, although many of the poorest families live in privately rented accommodation. Similarly, the previous Labour government were apparently quite content to see council house rents rise sharply while many local councils either had no rent rebate scheme at all or an inadequate scheme.

The **Local Government Act** brought about the first major reform of local government in England and Wales for 80 years. It created a two-tier structure of local government replacing 1,245 then existing local councils by less than 400. The broad aim of this Act was to see, as far as practicable, that the new local authority areas were related to areas within which people had a common interest – through living in a recognisable community, or through the link of employment.

The **Road Traffic (Foreign Vehicles) Act** represented one of the Government's measures taken to deal with the problem of heavy lorries, particularly those from foreign countries. It provided for effective enforcement of certain road traffic laws (e.g. those concerning vehicle weights) in respect of foreign goods vehicles and public service vehicles temporarily visiting Britain.

The **Transport (Grants) Act** provided for grants to be made to the British Railways Board and to the National Bus Company to assist those concerns in complying with their statutory financial obligations in the light of the Confederation of British Industry's initiative on price restraint.

The **Transport Holding Company Act** empowered the government to sell Thomas Cook and Son Limited to the private sector and to dissolve the Transport Holding Company. Thomas Cook was subsequently disposed of to private enterprise.

The **Town and Country Planning (Amendment) Act** enabled local authorities to work jointly in the preparation of structure plans (which are the broad strategic plans for the area as a whole) and speeded up the process of planning in Greater London.

The **Deposit of Poisonous Waste Act** made it an offence punishable with heavy penalties to deposit poisonous, noxious or polluting wastes which were liable to give rise to an environmental hazard.

The **National Insurance Act** provided for all-round increases in the main Social Security benefits which gave these benefits their highest buying power ever. It also provided for the gradual extension of the Special Attendance Allowance at a lower rate to cover those chronically disabled people needing a good deal of care and attention day or night instead of both day and night as was originally the case. The weekly contributions were increased to help pay for these improvements but those earning £18 a week or less (average male industrial earnings were about £31.37 a week in October 1971) received all the increases provided by this Act without having to pay anything extra in contributions.

The **Pensioners and Family Income Supplement Payments Act** provided for the payment of what became known as a tax-free Christmas bonus of £10 for a single pensioner and £20 for a married couple, both of whom were over pensionable age. This Act also laid down that The Family Income Supplement (FIS) which was payable to low wage earning families with children, would be awarded for a period of a year irrespective of changes in family circumstances during that time; as well as reducing administrative costs this provision allowed more incentive for those families to earn more because they did not immediately lose their supplement.

The **Superannuation Act** provided for public service pensions to be reviewed annually in the light of changes in prices. Between mid-1971 and mid-1972 prices rose by only about 6 per cent and many occupational pension schemes were able to give their members good protection against inflation. This was because, unlike today, the income from pension funds was broadly keeping pace with rising prices.

The **British Library Act** established a National Library under the management of the British Library Board.

The **Maintenance Orders (Reciprocal Enforcement) Act** helped deserted wives to obtain their maintenance payments by making improved provision for the reciprocal enforcement of maintenance orders between Britain and certain other countries.

The **Criminal Justice Act** recognised that in some respects the Courts needed increased powers to deal adequately with those who committed certain crimes. Its main provisions were:

(i) increased penalties for certain offences involving fire-arms (which applied to Britain as a whole);

(ii) the strengthening of the powers of the Court to require criminals to pay compensation to their victims; under this Act it was made possible for the Courts to order an offender to pay compensation in respect of personal injury and loss or damage resulting from any offence for which he had been convicted or which were taken into consideration by the Courts in determining sentence;

(iii) the introduction of new forms of non-custodial punishment. These were (a) the performance of some form of community service during a criminal's spare time; (b) attendance at day training centres, the aim of which was to provide social education linked with intensive probation supervision on a more or less full time basis;

(iv) the introduction of a new concept of criminal bankruptcy; the purpose of this was to ensure that those guilty of major crimes were not able to benefit from the fruits of their criminal activities and the Courts were therefore empowered to make a criminal bankruptcy order in certain circumstances.

Scottish legislation included:

(*a*) The **Housing (Financial Provisions) (Scotland) Act** which made similar provisions as regards housing subsidies in Scotland to that made for England and Wales by the Housing Finance Act of this year. The Scottish Act naturally took account of special conditions in Scotland and therefore the fair rents system was not extended to council housing in Scotland; instead the Act provided for 'standard rents' based upon the revenue needed from rents to balance the local authority's housing revenue account.

(*b*) The **National Health Service (Scotland) Act** which reorganised the National Health Service in Scotland by bringing all the main branches of the service under one administrative roof with a single health board responsible for all administration in each area.

Conservative Private Members legislation included:

(1) The **Trade Description Act** which required certain imported goods to show the country of origin.

(2) The **Harbours, Piers and Ferries (Scotland) Act** which gave the Secretary of State power to authorise harbour improvements in Scotland costing up to £200,000 by local and harbour authorities.

(3) The **Affiliation Proceedings (Amendment) Act** which improved the legal rights of unmarried mothers.

(4) The **Social Work (Scotland) Act** which ensured that child offenders becoming 16 during their appearance before a children's hearing (the system which replaced juvenile courts in Scotland for those under 16) would continue to be dealt with by the system of children's hearings as if they were under 16.

1973

The proposals contained in Mr Barber's third Budget were embodied in the **Finance Act** of this year. This Budget was firmly set in the context of economic growth and the Chancellor was able to report that over the past year the economy had been growing in line with the Government's target of 5 per cent a year growth.

The second major factor determining the proposals in this Budget was the need to maintain reasonable price stability, and this was helped by the substitution of Value Added Tax for Purchase Tax and the Selective Employment Tax. The then 10 per cent standard rate of Value Added Tax was the lowest in Europe and by April 1973 the Conservative government had reduced taxes on spending by about £900m., so making a major contribution to stable prices.

Apart from the introduction of Value Added Tax, there were a number of other tax changes including:
 (i) improvements in the special tax allowances for the elderly;
 (ii) the easing of the rule under which, for estate duty purposes, assets must be valued at the date of death. This rule could cause considerable hardship where there was a fall in the price of shares after the death, and this unfairness was dealt with;
 (iii) a Land Hoarding Charge designed to prevent excessive profits being made from land transactions; the charge was to be levied where there was failure to start permitted development within a reasonable time.

In addition the Budget contained a number of measures to encourage savings, for example new types of National Savings were started and the permitted maximum holdings of National Savings Certificates were increased.

The **Counter-Inflation Act** provided for the setting up of two new agencies, the Price Commission and the Pay Board, and empowered the Government and these new agencies to regulate prices, pay and dividends for three years. The Government's view was that, with inflation becoming a major problem in other countries as well as in Britain, it would be a long-term task to ensure price stability. Provision was made for the powers taken under this Act to be terminated within the three year period if it was found possible to obtain voluntary agreement on adequate arrangements. For the Government's intention was that the machinery provided for by this Act could be used under voluntary arrangements where these could be agreed.

The **Coal Industry Act** provided special help for miners made redundant by the contraction of the coal industry.

The **Concorde Aircraft Act** provided financial assistance from the Exchequer for the production of Concorde.

The **Employment and Training Act** implemented the Government's proposals for the reorganisation and improvement of industrial training. Its main provisions were:
 (i) The establishment of the Manpower Services Commission and the Employment Service Agency and the Training Services Agency. The agencies were intended as executive arms of the Manpower Services Commission, who would have responsibility over the whole field of industrial training.

(ii) The government was empowered to provide temporary employment for unemployed people through arrangements such as the Community Industry Scheme for out of work teenagers.

(iii) This Act required local authorities to provide a Careers Service, and modified the Industrial Training Act 1964, limiting training levies and exempting small firms and those with adequate training arrangements.

This Act was the culmination of a period in which there had been considerable expansion of industrial training with, for example, the doubling of expenditure on industrial training in the first three years of Conservative government.

The **Fair Trading Act** provided for the appointment of a Director-General of Fair Trading, made better provision for the protection of consumers and strengthened the law on monopolies, mergers and restrictive practices. The Act broke new ground in the field of consumer protection. Under this Act the Director-General, on the advice of a Consumer Protection Advisory Committee, was empowered to recommend the government to place Orders before Parliament which would outlaw practices considered unfair and harmful to consumers.

The provisions of the Act for strengthening the law on monopolies included one which enabled a reference to be made to the Monopolies Commission on any alleged abuse of their monopoly power by the nationalised industries.

The **Supply of Goods (Implied Terms) Act** prevented the consumer from having his legal rights undermined by the small print on an order form or by so-called guarantees. Although the buyer had always had certain rights both in common law and under the Sales of Goods Act 1893, it had, until this Act became law, been possible to limit or nullify these rights by phoney guarantees or exclusion clauses in the contract of sale. This Act remedied this abuse.

The **Insurance Companies Amendment Act** was passed in the light of public concern following the collapse of the Vehicle and General Insurance company. The Act improved certain of the existing safeguards for the protection of the policy holder and introduced new requirements to facilitate his understanding of the policies offered. In this way, the competitive edge of the insurance industry has been maintained while the interests of the consumer have been given greater protection.

The **Furnished Lettings (Rent Allowances) Act** extended the provision of rent allowances started under the Housing Finance Acts to all families in need living in furnished privately rented homes. As a result it was now the case that any family in need, whether they lived in council housing or privately rented accommodation, furnished or unfurnished, could get help with the rent; no family need fear eviction because of being unable to afford the rent. So security of tenure was considerably strengthened.

The **Housing Amendment Act** extended by one year from June 1973 the scheme launched under the Housing Act 1971 to provide special assistance with the improvement of older houses in development areas where the need was greatest.

The **Land Compensation Act** provided improved compensation for those whose property had either been compulsorily purchased or adversely affected or blighted by road and redevelopment schemes.

This Act reflected the Government's belief that, although a balance had to be struck between the needs for essential development in the interests of the community as a whole and the need to protect the rights of owners of property who may be injured by such development, this balance had been tilted too heavily against individual people adversely affected by development.

This Act, therefore, contained a number of provisions which strengthened the rights of the individual. First, it was provided that an occupier, whether as owner or tenant, was able to get a special home loss payment in addition to any entitlement to normal market value payment where the house in which he was living was compulsorily purchased, if he had lived in the house as his main or only home for at least five years.

Second, the Act gave a new right to advance payments of compensation of up to 90 per cent of the amount estimated by the acquiring authority. This helped home owners or owners of businesses or farms who wanted immediate money to enable them to buy other property where there was a delay in settling the amount of compensation due.

Third, a new statutory duty was placed on Housing Authorities to rehouse residential occupiers displaced by compulsory purchase where there was no suitable alternative accommodation otherwise available on reasonable terms. This replaced the previous varying legal obligations. The Act also put a legal bar upon the practice of reducing the amount of compensation payable where a local council rehouse a person in a council house.

Fourth, the Act provided a better deal for small businesses by providing that their right to a renewal of tenancy was taken into account in assessing the amount of any compensation; the Act also gave certain business tenants a right for the first time to compensation for trade loss and to removal expenses.

Fifth, those whose property had become virtually unsaleable (blighted) because of possible development were given improved and extended rights to require the authority to buy their property at the market price *before* it had become blighted.

The **Water Act** reorganised the water services in England and Wales on a basis of ten all-purpose regional water authorities (including the Welsh National Water Development Authority) which became competent to deal with water supply and conservation; pollution control and monitoring; sewerage and sewage disposal; and recreation amenity uses of water.

The **National Insurance and Supplementary Benefit Act** provided for improvements in pensions and other national insurance benefits. This was the third time pensions and benefits had been improved since the Conservatives took office in June 1970. When the increases provided for under this Act started in October 1973, the pension was 55 per cent higher than in June 1970 – an increase well ahead of prices and broadly in line with average industrial earnings.

This Act also provided for a tax free Christmas 'Bonus' of £10 for a single pensioner and £20 for a married couple, both of whom were over pensionable age, to be paid in November of this year.

The **Social Security Act** made a number of improvements in the basic National Insurance scheme. First, it gave statutory backing to the annual review of pensions which had taken place under this Conservative government. Second, it provided for pensions and benefits to be financed by means of a completely earnings related contribution up to a certain earnings ceiling; this had two advantages:

(*a*) It ensured a buoyant revenue which increased automatically as earnings rose and

(*b*) it was more fair in that low wage earners no longer paid a disproportionately high share of the cost of benefits.

Thirdly, it provided that over the years, all employed people would be covered by a second and earnings related pension on top of their basic state pension. It was intended that most people would be catered for by good occupational schemes, but the Act made provision for a reserve state scheme for those who could not be adequately covered in any other way.

The Act also provided for pension rights in occupational schemes to be properly protected on change of job. There had been a big increase in the number of employed people covered by occupational schemes since the passing of the Conservative National Insurance Act 1959 which provided for additions over and above the basic state pension to be paid in return for a graduated element in the weekly contribution, except in the case of those covered by contracted out occupational schemes; between the end of 1958 and the end of 1976 the number of people covered by occupational schemes rose from $8\frac{3}{4}$ million to about $11\frac{1}{2}$ million which is equivalent to roughly half the employed population.

The **National Health Service Reorganisation Act** unified hospital, general practitioner and local personal health services in England and Wales into a single administrative structure. Regional Health authorities were made responsible for overall planning and financial allocation; while Area Health Authorities became the main administrative bodies. Provision was made for the setting up of Community Health Councils to represent consumer opinion and report to the Area Health Authorities. The Act also provided for the appointment of a National Health Service Commissioner (ombudsman) to investigate complaints from the general public.

The Government's view was that with all three branches of the National Health Service brought under one administrative roof, it would be easier to ensure that resources were distributed in accordance with proper priorities.

The **Education (Work Experience) Act** enabled children in their last year of compulsory schooling to obtain work experience as part of their education. Previously, only children over compulsory leaving age could take part in this scheme.

The **Guardianship Act** gave mothers equal rights with fathers over the guardianship of their children, where previously the father's rights were paramount.

The **Fire Precautions (Loans) Act** extended the limited loans scheme under the Fire Precautions Act 1971, by empowering local authorities to make loans at their discretion to persons with premises which are required to have fire certificates under the 1971 Act.

Scottish legislation included:

(*a*) The **Land Compensation (Scotland) Act** which applied to Scotland provisions of the Act passed earlier this year affecting England and Wales.

(*b*) The **Local Government (Scotland) Act** which reformed local government in Scotland on the lines provided for in England and Wales by the Local Government Act 1972.

Conservative Private Members legislation included:

(1) The **Employment Agencies Act** which lay down standards of conduct for employment agencies and required private employment agencies to obtain licences from local councils.

(2) The **Hallmarking Act** which established a British Hallmarking Council and tightened up existing standards.

(3) The **Heavy Commercial Vehicles (Controls and Regulations) Act** which provided for certain controls on heavy commercial vehicles including the empowering of traffic authorities to prescribe routes to be followed by these vehicles.

(4) The **Dentists (Amendment) Act** which tightened up on the registration procedure for dentists, in order to ensure that foreign dentists with inadequate qualifications could not practise in this country.

(5) The **Employment of Children Act** which replaced the arrange-

ments whereby local authorities in Britain could make by-laws regarding the employment of children of school age, by empowering the government to make arrangements on a uniform basis over the whole country.

(6) The **Domicile and Matrimonial Proceedings Act** which provided that a married woman living separately from her husband could, if she wished, have a separate domicile of her own.

(7) The **Succession (Scotland) Act** which improved the financial provisions relating to rights of the surviving spouse in Scotland.

1974

Although the General Election, which resulted in the return of the Labour government, took place in February of this year, a number of important measures received the Royal Assent before the dissolution of Parliament.

The **Local Government Act** contained a number of important provisions regarding rates and local government finance generally. First, it relieved the burden on ratepayers. When the Health Service was reorganised under the National Health Service Reorganisation Act 1973 local councils were no longer responsible for administering local health services and were, therefore, relieved of the cost of these services.

Under the **Local Government Act** of this year, local councils were relieved of 90 per cent of the cost of mandatory grants to students; rate rebates were improved so that they became comparable with rent rebates with 90 per cent of the cost of these improved rebates met by the Exchequer.

Disabled people were exempted from rates in respect of any land used for garages, and people no longer became subject to immediate increases in rates because they had made minor improvements to their homes or installed central heating. Under this Act liability for increased rates in respect of such improvements did not arise until there was a general revaluation of property for rating purposes. The allowances for repairs and maintenance which had the effect of reducing liability for rates were improved as a result of which some 10 million home owners had their rates reduced by amounts ranging from £1 to £10 a year.

The distribution arrangements for the Exchequer Rates Support Grant to local councils were improved in order to give more help to the problem areas of cities. But at the same time the special assistance designed to keep down household rates generally was increased so that people living in other parts of the country would not suffer as a result of the extra help for the cities.

The Act discontinued a number of specific grants covering a range of transport and highway functions and substituted a block grant. The aim was to encourage a comprehensive approach in dealing with public transport, highways, the regulation of traffic and parking provisions. In addition the Act provided more sensible and flexible arrangements for the rating of empty property.

Finally, the Act provided for an ombudsman system for investigating complaints about local government.

The **Biological Weapons Act** enabled Britain to ratify the Biological Weapons Convention. The purpose of this Convention was to ban the possession in all circumstances of biological and toxin weapons, and the aim of this Act was to make specific provision in British Law to satisfy this obligation.

APPENDIX

The principal Conservative industrial and social Acts: 1800 to 1974

	page
Abandonment of Animals Act (1960)	75
Abnormal Importations Act (1931)	37
Administration of Estates Act (1925)	31
Adoption of Children Act (1926)	32
Adoption of Children (Regulation) Act (1939)	43
Advertisements (Hire-Purchase) Act (1957)	68
Affiliation Orders Act (1952)	60
Affiliation Proceedings (Amendment) Act (1972)	106
Agricultural Credits Act (1923)	28
Agricultural Credits Act (1928)	34
Agricultural Marketing Act (1933)	38
Agricultural Produce (Grading and Marketing) Act (1928)	34
Agricultural Wages (Regulation) Amendment Act (1940)	44
Agricultural Act (1936)	40
Agricultural Act (1937)	41
Agricultural Act (1957)	67
Agriculture Act (1958)	69
Agriculture and Horticulture Act (1964)	87
Agriculture (Miscellaneous Provisions) Act (1944)	51
Agriculture (Miscellaneous Provisions) Act (1963)	83
Agriculture (Safety, Health and Welfare Provisions) Act (1956)	65
Agriculture (Small Farmers) Act (1959)	71
Air Guns and Shot Guns, Etc., Act (1962)	81
Allotments Act (1887)	21
Animal Boarding Establishments Act (1963)	85
Animal (Cruel Poisons) Act (1962)	81
Artisans' Dwellings Act (1875)	18
Atomic Energy Act (1971)	97
Atomic Energy Authority Act (1954)	62
Baking Industry (Hours of Work) Act (1954)	62
Betting and Gaming Act (1960)	75
Betting Levy Act (1961)	78
Biological Weapons Act (1974)	113
Blind Persons Act (1920)	27
Blind Persons Act (1938)	42
British Library Act (1972)	105

Cancer Act (1939)	page 43
Caravan Sites and Control of Development Act (1960)	74
Carriage of Goods by Sea Act (1971)	101
Charities Act (1960)	74
Catering Wages Act (1943)	46
Children Act (1958)	69
Children and Young Persons Act (1932)	38
Children and Young Persons Act (1933)	38
Children and Young Persons Act (1938)	42
Children and Young Persons Act (1963)	83
Children and Young Persons (Harmful Publications) Act (1955)	64
Cinematograph Films Act (1927)	34
Civil Aviation Act (1971)	98
Civil Aviation (Licensing) Act (1960)	73
Clean Air Act (1956)	66
Coal Industry Act (1956)	65
Coal Industry Act (1971)	97
Coal Industry Act (1973)	107
Coal Mining (Subsidence) Act (1957)	67
Coal Regulations Act (1842)	11
Common Lodging-Houses Act (1851)	13
Commonwealth Immigrants Act (1962)	80
Companies (Floating Charges) (Scotland) Act (1961)	78
Concorde Aircraft Act (1973)	107
Conspiracy Act (1875)	18
Consumer Protection Act (1971)	101
Contracts of Employment Act (1963)	82
Corneal Grafting Act (1952)	60
Cotton Act (1954)	62
Cotton Cloth Factory Act (1889)	21
Cotton Industry Act (1923)	29
Cotton Industry Act (1959)	71
Cotton Industry (Reorganisation) Act (1939)	43
Counter-Inflation Act (1973)	107
Counter-Inflation (Temporary Provisions) Act (1972)	103
Covent Garden Market Act (1961)	76
Criminal Appeal Act (1964)	88
Criminal Damage Act (1971)	100
Criminal Justice Act (1961)	77
Criminal Justice Act (1972)	105
Criminal Justice Administration Act (1962)	80
Criminal Justice (Scotland) Act (1963)	85
Customs Duties (Dumping and Subsidies) Act (1957)	67
Dangerous Drugs and Poisons (Amendment) Act (1923)	29
Deer Act (1963)	85

Principal Conservative Acts 1800 to 1974 | 117

Dentists Act (1956)	page 66
Dentists (Amendment) Act (1973)	111
Deposit of Poisonous Waste Act (1972)	104
Determination of Needs Act (1941)	45
Determination of Needs Act (1943)	46
Disabled Persons (Employment) Act (1944)	50
Distribution of Industry Act (1945)	52
Distribution of Industry (Industrial Finance) Act (1958)	69
Dock Workers (Pension) Act (1960)	73
Domicile and Matrimonial Proceedings Act (1973)	112
Drugs (Prevention of Misuse) Act (1964)	88
Education Act (1876)	19
Education Act (1902)	24
Education Act (1918)	26
Education Act (1926)	31
Education Act (1936)	40
Education Act (1944)	49
Education Act (1959)	72
Education Act (1962)	80
Education Act (1964)	87
Education (Handicapped Children) Act (1970)	95
Education (Miscellaneous Provisions) Act (1953)	61
Education (Scotland) Act (1963)	84
Education (Scotland) Act (1971)	101
Education (Work Experience) Act (1973)	111
Electricity Act (1926)	32
Electricity Act (1957)	67
Electricity Reorganisation (Scotland) Act (1954)	62
Employers' and Workmen's Act (1875)	17
Employment Agencies Act (1973)	111
Employment and Training Act (1973)	107
Employment Medical Advisory Service Act (1971)	102
Employment of Children Act (1973)	111
Employment of Women and Children Act (1920)	27
Equal Franchise Act (1928)	35
Equalisation of Subsidies Housing (Financial Provisions) Act (1938)	42
Export Guarantees Act (1945)	52
Export Guarantees Act (1952)	60
Factories Act (1874)	17
Factories Act (1937)	41
Factories and Workshop Act (1901)	23
Factory and Workshop Act (1891)	22
Fair Trading Act (1973)	108

Family Allowances Act (1945)	page 52
Family Allowances and National Insurance Act (1952)	60
Family Allowances and National Insurance Act (1956)	65
Family Allowances and National Insurance Act (1961)	76
Family Allowances and National Insurance Act (1964)	87
Family Income Supplements Act (1970)	95
Finance Act (1952)	59
Finance Act (1953)	61
Finance Act (1954)	62
Finance Acts (1955)	64
Finance Act (1956)	65
Finance Act (1957)	67
Finance Act (1958)	69
Finance Act (1959)	70
Finance Act (1960)	73
Finance Act (1961)	75
Finance Act (1962)	78
Finance Act (1963)	81
Finance Act (1964)	85
Finance Act (1971)	96
Finance Act (1972)	101
Finance Act (1973)	106
Fire Precaution (Loans) Act (1973)	111
Fire Precautions Act (1971)	100
Flood Prevention (Scotland) Act (1961)	78
Food and Drugs Act (1955)	64
Food and Drugs Amendment Act (1954)	63
Food and Drugs (Milk and Dairies) Act (1944)	51
Food and Drugs (Scotland) Act (1956)	66
Forestry Act (1945)	53
Fort William Pulp and Paper Mills Act (1963)	82
Friendly Societies Act (1875)	19
Furnished Lettings (Rent Allowances) Act (1973)	108
Guardianship Act (1973)	111
Guardianship of Infants Act (1925)	31
Hairdressers (Registration) Act (1964)	88
Hallmarking Act (1973)	111
Harbours Act (1964)	86
Harbours (Amendment) Act (1970)	96
Harbours (Loans) Act (1972)	103
Harbours, Piers and Ferries (Scotland) Act (1972)	106
Heating Appliances (Fireguards) Act (1952)	60
Health Visiting and Social Work (Training) Act (1962)	79

Principal Conservative Acts 1800 to 1974 | 119

	page
Heavy Commercial Vehicles (Controls and Regulations) Act (1973)	111
Herring Industry Act (1944)	51
Highways Act (1971)	99
Hijacking Act (1971)	100
Hire-Purchase Act (1938)	42
Hire-Purchase Act (1964)	87
Holidays With Pay Act (1938)	42
Home Safety Act (1961)	78
Horticulture Act (1960)	73
Hospital Endowment (Scotland) Act (1971)	101
House of Commons (Redistribution of Seats) Act (1944)	52
House Purchase and Housing Act (1959)	71
Housing Act (1923)	28
Housing Act (1935)	40
Housing Act (1961)	77
Housing Act (1964)	87
Housing Act (1971)	98
Housing Amendment Act (1973)	109
Housing and Town Development (Scotland) Act (1957)	68
Housing Finance Act (1972)	103
Housing (Financial Provisions) Act (1933)	38
Housing (Financial Provisions) Act (1938)	42
Housing (Financial Provisions) (Scotland) Act (1972)	106
Housing of the Working Classes Act (1890)	21
Housing (Repairs and Rents) Act (1954)	63
Housing (Repairs and Rents) (Scotland) Act (1954)	63
Housing (Rural Workers) Acts (1944)	50
Housing (Scotland) Act (1962)	80
Housing Subsidies Act (1956)	66
Housing (Temporary Accommodation) Act (1944)	50
Housing (Temporary Provisions) Act (1944)	50
Human Tissue Act (1961)	77
Immigration Act (1971)	100
Import Duties Act (1932)	37
Income Tax Act (1945)	53
Income Tax (Repayment of Post-War Credits) Act (1959)	70
Industrial and Provident Societies Act (1928)	35
Industrial Diseases (Benefit) Act (1954)	63
Industrial Insurance Act (1923)	28
Industrial Relations Act (1971)	98
Industrial Training Act (1964)	85
Industry Act (1971)	98
Industry Act (1972)	102
Insurance Companies Amendment Act (1973)	108

International Monetary Fund Act (1962)	page 79
Investment and Building Grants Act (1971)	97
Iron and Steel Act (1953)	61
Land Commission (Dissolution) Act (1971)	99
Land Compensation Act (1973)	109
Land Compensation (Scotland) Act (1973)	111
Landlord and Tenant Act (1927)	34
Landlord and Tenant Act (1954)	63
Landlord and Tenant Act (1962)	81
Landlord and Tenant (Furniture and Fittings) Act (1959)	72
Law Reform (Husband and Wife) Act (1962)	81
Lead Paint (Protection Against Poisoning) Act (1926)	32
Legal Aid Act (1960)	74
Legitimacy Act (1926)	32
Licensed Premises in New Towns Act (1952)	60
Licensing Act (1961)	77
Licensing (Scotland) Act (1962)	80
Litter Act (1958)	70
Livestock Industry Act (1937)	42
Local Authorities (Expenditure on Special Purposes) (Scotland) Act (1961)	78
Local Employment Act (1960)	73
Local Employment Act (1963)	82
Local Government Act (1888)	21
Local Government Act (1929)	35
Local Government Act (1958)	69
Local Government Act (1972)	104
Local Government Act (1974)	112
Local Government and Miscellaneous Financial Provisions (Scotland) Act (1958)	69
Local Government (Financial Provisions, Etc.) (Scotland) Act (1962)	81
Local Government (Scotland) Act (1973)	111
Lodging-Houses Act (1851)	14
London Government Act (1963)	84
London Passenger Transport Act (1933)	39
Long Leases (Scotland) Act (1954)	63
Lotteries and Gaming Act (1962)	81
Maintenance Order (Reciprocal Enforcement) Act (1972)	105
Maintenance Orders Act (1958)	70
Marketing Act (1933)	39
Malicious Damage Act (1964)	88
Marriage (Enabling) Act (1960)	75
Master and Servant Act (1867)	16

Maternity and Child Welfare Act (1918)	page 26
Mental Deficiency Act (1927)	33
Mental Health Act (1959)	71
Mental Health (Scotland) Act (1960)	74
Merchant Shipping Act (1876)	19
Merchant Shipping (International Labour Convention) Act (1925)	31
Merchant Shipping (Oil Pollution) Act (1971)	98
Midwives Act (1936)	40
Midwives and Maternity Homes Act (1926)	32
Milk Act (1934)	39
Milk and Dairies Order (1926)	32
Mineral Workings (Offshore Installations) Act (1971)	98
Mines and Quarries Act (1954)	62
Mines Regulation Act (1887)	20
Mining Industry Act (1926)	32
Mining Royalties Act (1938)	42
Ministry of Health Act (1919)	27
Ministry of National Insurance Act (1944)	48
Misuse of Drugs Act (1971)	100
Monopolies and Restrictive Practices Commission Act (1953)	61
Motor Vehicles (Passenger Insurance) Act (1971)	101
National Assistance Act (1959)	71
National Health Insurance Act (1928)	35
National Health Insurance (Juvenile Contributors and Young Persons) Act (1937)	41
National Health Insurance and Contributory Pensions Act (1935)	40
National Health Insurance, Contributory Pensions and Workmen's Compensation Act (1941)	45
National Health Service Act (1952)	60
National Health Service Reorganisation Act (1973)	110
National Health Service (Scotland) Act (1972)	106
National Insurance Act (1953)	61
National Insurance Act (1954)	62
National Insurance Act (1956)	67
National Insurance Act (1957)	67
National Insurance (No 2) Act (1957)	68
National Insurance Act (1959)	71
National Insurance Act (1960)	74
National Insurance Act (1963)	83
National Insurance Act (1970)	94
National Insurance Act (1971)	99
National Insurance Act (1972)	104
National Insurance and Supplementary Benefit Act (1973)	110

National Insurance (Industrial Injuries) Act (1953) page 61
New Towns Act (1959) 72
Noise Abatement Act (1960) 75
Nuclear Installations (Licensing and Insurance) Act (1959) 70
Nurses Act (1943) 46
Nursing Homes Registration Act (1927) 33

Obscene Publications Act (1964) 88
Old Age Pensions Act (1919) 27
Old Age and Widows' Pensions Act (1940) 44
Offices, Shops and Railway Premises Act (1963) 82
Oil Burners (Standard) Act (1960) 75
Oil in Navigable Waters Act (1971) 98
Opticians Act (1958) 70
Ottawa Agreements Act (1932) 37

Parliament (Qualification of Women) Act (1918) 27
Payment of Wages Act (1960) 73
Pensioners and Family Income Supplement Payments Act (1972) 105
Pensions (Increase) Act (1944) 51
Pensions (Increase) Act (1952) 60
Pensions (Increase) Act (1956) 66
Pensions (Increase) Act (1959) 71
Pensions (Increase) Act (1962) 79
Pensions (Increase) Act (1971) 99
Physical Training and Recreation Act (1937) 41
Physical Training and Recreation Act (1958) 70
Pneumoconiosis and Byssinosis Benefit Act (1952) 60
Police Act (1964) 88
Police, Fire and Probation Officers Remuneration Act (1956) 66
Poor Law (Amendment) Act (1938) 42
Prevention of Crime Act (1953) 61
Professions Supplementary to Medicine Act (1960) 74
Protection of Animals (Anaesthetics) Act (1964) 88
Protection of Depositors (1963) 83
Public Bodies (Admission to Meetings) Act (1960) 75
Public Health Act (1875) 17
Public Health Act (1925) 31
Public Health Act (1961) 76
Public Health (Scotland) Act (1867) 16
Public Order Act (1963) 84

Radioactive Substances Act (1960) 74
Rating Act (1971) 99

Rating and Valuation Act (1961) page 77
Reform Act (1867) 16
Refreshment Houses Act (1964) 88
Reinstatement in Civil Employment Act (1944) 50
Rent Act (1957) 68
Rent Restriction Act (1923) 28
Rent Restriction Act (1938) 42
Representation of the People Act (1918) 26
Representation of the People Act (1945) 54
Resale Prices Act (1964) 86
Requisitioned Houses and Housing (Amendment) Act (1955) 64
Restrictive Trade Practices Act (1956) 65
Rights of Entry (Gas and Electricity Boards) Act (1954) 63
Road Traffic Act (1934) 39
Road Traffic Act (1956) 66
Road Traffic Act (1962) 79
Road and Rail Traffic Act (1933) 39
Road Traffic and Roads Improvement Act (1960) 74
Road Traffic (Foreign Vehicles) Act (1972) 104
Rolls Royce Purchase Act (1971) 98
Royal Irish Constabulary (Widows' Pensions) Act (1954) 63
Rural Housing Act (1926) 32
Rural Water Supplies and Sewerage Act (1944) 51

Safeguarding of Industries Act (1921) 27
Sale of Food and Drugs Act (1875) 17
School Crossing Patrols Act (1953) 61
Separation and Maintenance Act (1925) 31
Sex Disqualification (Removal) Act (1919) 27
Shipbuilding Credit Act (1964) 86
Shipping Contracts and Commercial Documents Act (1964) 86
Shop Act (1934) 39
Shop Hours Regulation Act (1892) 22
Shops Act (1904) 24
Shops (Hours of Closing) Act (1928) 35
Small Holdings Act (1892) 22
Small Holdings and Allotments Act (1926) 32
Social Security Act (1971) 99
Social Security Act (1973) 110
Social Work (Scotland) Act (1972) 106
Special Areas (Development and Improvement) Act (1934) 39
Street Offences Act (1959) 72
Succession (Scotland) Act (1973) 112
Suicide Act (1961) 77
Superannuation Act (1972) 105
Supply of Goods (Implied Terms) Act (1973) 108

Teachers' (Superannuation) Act (1945)	page 53
Teachers' (Superannuation) Act (1954)	63
Teachers' (Superannuation) Act (1956)	66
Television Act (1954)	63
Television Act (1963)	84
Ten Hours Act (1847)	13
Town and Country Planning Act (1944)	51
Town and Country Planning Act (1959)	72
Town and Country Planning (Amendment) Act (1972)	104
Trade Description Act (1972)	106
Trade Disputes and Trade Unions Act (1927)	32
Trade Facilities Act (1921)	28
Trade Union (Amalgamations Etc.) Act (1964)	88
Transitional Payments (Determination of Need) Act (1932)	38
Transport Act (1953)	61
Transport Act (1962)	79
Transport (Grants) Act (1972)	104
Transport Holding Company Act (1972)	104
Tribunals and Inquiries Act (1958)	70
Truck Acts (1831)	10
Truck Amendment Act (1887)	21
Trustees Investments Act (1961)	76
Trusts (Scotland) Act (1961)	78
Tuberculosis Order (1926)	32
Unemployed Workmen Act (1905)	24
Unemployment Act (1934)	39
Unemployment Insurance Act (1920)	27
Unemployment Insurance Act (1927)	33
Unemployment Insurance Act (1939)	43
Unemployment Insurance Act (1940)	44
Unemployment Insurance (Increase of Benefit) Act (1944)	51
Unsolicited Goods and Services Act (1971)	101
Voluntary Pensions Act (1937)	41
Wages Councils Act (1945)	53
Water Act (1945)	53
Water Act (1958)	69
Water Act (1973)	110
Water Resources Act (1963)	84
Water Resources Act (1971)	99
Weights and Measures Act (1963)	82
Wheat Act (1932)	37
Widows' and Orphans' and Old Age Pensions Act (1925)	30
Workmen's Compensation Act (1897)	22

Principal Conservative Acts 1800 to 1974 | 125

Workmen's Compensation Act (1923) *page* 28
Workmen's Compensation Act (1943) 46
Workmen's Compensation and Benefit (Supplementation) Act (1956) 66
Workmen's Compensation (Amendment) Act (1900) 23
Workmen's Compensation (Amendment) Act (1938) 42
Workmen's Compensation (Coal Mines) Act (1934) 40
Workmen's Compensation (Supplementary Allowances) Act (1940) 44
Workmen's Compensation (Temporary Increases) Act (1943) 46
Workmen's Compensation and Benefit (Byssinosis) Act (1940) 44

Young Persons (Employment) Act (1938) 42
Young Persons Employment Act (1964) 88

Index of persons

Addington, Henry, 9
Anderson, Sir John, 53
Asquith, Herbert, 24, 25, 62
Attlee, Clement, 55

Baldwin, Stanley, 28, 29, 30, 31, 41
Balfour, Arthur, 22
Barber, Anthony (now Lord), 91, 96, 97, 101, 106
Barnes, G. W., 23
Bevan, Aneurin, 47, 57
Beveridge, Sir William, 48
Bevin, Ernest, 53
Blanesburgh, Lord, 33
Bondfield, Margaret, 33
Bowerman, C. W., 23
Bright, John, 12, 13
Brown, Colonel Clifton, 52
Burt, Thomas, 21
Butler, R. A. (now Lord), 49, 59, 61, 62, 64

Callaghan, James, 85
Campbell, J. R., 30
Campbell-Bannerman, Sir Henry, 24
Chamberlain, Joseph, 19, 25
Chamberlain, Neville, 28, 30, 41
Chaplin, Henry, 25
Churchill, Winston, 25, 30, 46, 48, 53, 55, 62
Cobden, Richard, 13
Cripps, Sir Stafford, 55
Crooks, Will, 24
Cross, Richard, 17, 18
Crossman, Richard, 56, 93

Derby, Lord, 14, 15, 19
Dickens, Charles, 12, 13
Disraeli, Benjamin (later Lord Beaconsfield), 10, 16, 17, 18, 19
Douglas-Home, Sir Alec (Lord Home), 55

Eden, Sir Anthony, 55

Fawcett, Henry, 19
Forster, W. M., 16

Gladstone, William, 16, 17, 20, 22

Hadow, Sir Henry, 32
Heath, Edward, 103
Heathcoat Amory, Derick (now Lord), 69, 70, 73
Hetherington, Sir Hector, 42
Houghton, Douglas (now Lord), 71
Huntley, T. W., 40

Jay, Douglas, 85
Jenkin, Patrick, 102
Joseph, Sir Keith, 77, 93

Kingsley, Charles, 18

Law, Bonar, 28
Liverpool, Lord, 9
Lloyd George, David, 25, 26, 28
Lloyd, Selwyn (now Lord Selwyn-Lloyd), 75, 76, 78, 79

Macdonald, A., 20
MacDonald, Ramsay, 24, 28, 29, 36
Macmillan, Harold, 55, 65
Maudling, Reginald, 81, 85
Morrison, Herbert, 57

Neave, Airey, 95
Nicholson, Godfrey, 40
Nightingale, Florence, 14

Odger, George, 18

Peel, Sir Robert, 10, 11, 12, 13
Perring, Sir W., 34

Index of persons

Rathbone, Eleanor, 35
Ritchie, C. T., 23
Rosebery, Earl of, 22

Sadler, Michael, 10
Salisbury, Lord, 20, 21, 22
Samuel, Sir Herbert, 37
Shaftesbury, Earl of, 11, 12, 13, 14, 18, 62
Shaw, Tom, 29
Streatfeild, Mr Justice, 80

Thatcher, Margaret, 75, 93, 95, 96
Thomas, S. A., 23
Thorneycroft, Peter (now Lord), 67
Tomlinson, George, 37

Warnock, Professor Mary, 96
Webb, Sidney and Beatrice, 10, 18
Willink, H. U., 47
Wilson, Harold (now Sir), 56
Woodcock, George, 85